From Jerusalem

to Zarahemla

The Exodus of Lehi's Family to Their Promised Land

By

Cooper Neitzel

content within this book has been derived from various sources. The views expressed herein are the sole responsibility of the author and do not necessarily reflect the position of The Church of Jesus Christ of Latter-day Saints.

By reading this document, the reader agrees that under no circumstances is the author responsible for any losses, direct or indirect, that are incurred as a result of the use of the information contained within this document, including, but not limited to, errors, omissions, or inaccuracies.

Library of Congress Control Number: 2024919560

Published by Hemingway Publishers

Cover design by Hemingway Publishers

ISBN: Printed in the United States

Table Of Contents

From Jerusalem to Zarahemla

The Exodus of Lehi's Family to Their Promised Land

This book examines the characters portrayed in the Small Plates of Nephi and the Brass Plates within the Book of Mormon, exploring their historical contexts, personal attributes, lessons learned, and spiritual teachings, accompanied by personal reflections. As the second installment in a three-book series, following 'Pathways to Promised Lands,' this work continues the exploration of pivotal figures in the Book of Mormon. This work offers in-depth biographical sketches and examines how each character's personal journey contributes to the overarching narratives of Nephite and Lamanite histories and the ultimate restoration of the Gospel of Jesus Christ.

The characters explored in this work are intended to deepen our appreciation of the divine purposes God has for all His children. To fully grasp these lessons, regular, direct engagement with the Book of Mormon is encouraged, as it enriches understanding through the guidance of the Holy Ghost. By engaging directly with the Book of Mormon, we can not only enrich our comprehension and deepen our spiritual insights but also connect more profoundly

1

with the experiences and teachings of these ancient figures, making their lessons more relevant to our own lives.

Part I

Prophets and Patriarchs - The

Foundation of Faith

Part I lays the foundation by exploring the pivotal figures whose faith and leadership established the spiritual and cultural bedrock of the Nephite and Lamanite civilizations. These three chapters delve into the lives of Lehi's family, examining their internal conflicts and the critical alliances they formed with key figures from Jerusalem, which were essential in shaping the early course of Nephite history. These chapters are integral to Part I as they illuminate the divine guidance, familial dynamics, and strategic partnerships that were crucial in shaping the early trajectory of Nephite history and faith.

Together, these chapters offer a comprehensive understanding of the individuals and dynamics that forged the foundation of Nephite faith and society. As we explore these stories, we are invited to reflect on the enduring principles of faith, leadership, and unity that continue to shape our spiritual journeys today. These chapters illustrate the vital roles of prophetic leadership, the consequences of internal dissent, and the strength gained through unity and alliances, setting the stage for the developments that would define Nephite history.

Chapter 1

The Prophetic Family

Lehi's journey, which marks the genesis of the Nephite and Lamanite civilizations, unfolds against the backdrop of Jerusalem's impending destruction—a pivotal narrative within the Book of Mormon. This chapter explores the lives and legacies of Lehi, Sariah, their sons—Nephi, Sam, Jacob, and Joseph—and their daughters, whose contributions were instrumental in establishing the spiritual and cultural foundations of their people. Each character plays a crucial role in the foundational narrative of leaving Jerusalem, journeying through the wilderness, and establishing a new society in the promised land.

Historical Context

Around 600 BC, Jerusalem was a city teetering on the brink of destruction. Prophets like Jeremiah warned of its impending fall due to the people's wickedness. In this volatile environment, while other prophets like Zedekiah warned of Jerusalem's destruction, Lehi received a unique command to not only prophesy but also to physically lead his family out of the city, beginning a journey that would shape the destiny of future civilizations (1 Nephi 1:4). This directive marked the beginning of a significant journey that would eventually lead them to the Americas, a land promised to them by the Lord.

Characters in Chapter 1

- **Lehi** ~ The visionary patriarch who led his family from Jerusalem, setting the spiritual tone for their journey.
- **Sariah** ~ The resilient matriarch who supported her family through trials, embodying unwavering faith.
- **Nephi** ~ The faithful and visionary son who exemplified leadership and obedience.
- **Sam** ~ The loyal and supportive brother whose quiet strength was crucial to the family's unity.
- **Jacob** ~ The prophet born in the wilderness, known for his teachings on justice and mercy.

- **Joseph** ~ The youngest son, whose prophetic legacy ties him to ancient and future prophecies.
- **Daughters of Lehi** ~ The silent pillars whose resilience and faith were essential in sustaining the family.

By examining these individuals, we gain insights into the foundational principles of faith, leadership, and resilience that characterized the early Nephite society. Their stories offer timeless lessons on the importance of following divine guidance and maintaining faith amidst adversity. In today's world, where challenges and uncertainties abound, their stories remind us of the unchanging importance of following divine guidance and maintaining unwavering faith, no matter the obstacles we face.

Lehi: Prophet and Patriarch in the Book of Mormon

Lehi, a prophet in the Book of Mormon **(1 Nephi 1:1-4)**, exemplifies several Christlike attributes that make him a significant figure in Latter-day Saint theology. Primarily, Lehi is a visionary man—a trait that aligns closely with prophetic insight and revelation, which are hallmarks of Christlike leadership. He was a visionary patriarch whose leadership not only set the spiritual tone for his family but also established the foundational principles that would guide future generations. His initial calling comes through a vision where he sees God surrounded by countless angels (1 Nephi 1:8). This vision marks the beginning of his prophetic ministry, demonstrating his openness to divine guidance.

Lehi's compassion and paternal care are evident as he warns the inhabitants of Jerusalem of their impending doom due to their wickedness, showing his concern for their spiritual welfare, much like Christ's lament over Jerusalem (1 Nephi 1:18-20). Throughout the narrative, Lehi's deep concern for his family's spiritual and temporal well-being drives many of his actions, mirroring the Savior's shepherding of His followers.

Moreover, Lehi's steadfastness and obedience are central to his character. Upon receiving the command to leave Jerusalem and take his family into the wilderness, he complies without hesitation, showing an unwavering faith similar to that of Abraham (1 Nephi 2:2-4). His commitment to following divine commandments, despite personal sacrifice, underscores a profound dedication to God's will.

Lessons and Teachings from Lehi's Life

Lehi's life and actions offer a wealth of lessons on faith, obedience, and divine reliance. From his prophetic call to his journey to the promised land, Lehi consistently demonstrates what it means to "live by every word that proceedeth out of the mouth of God" (Matthew 4:4).

The Power of Vision and Revelation

Lehi's experiences underscore the importance of seeking and following divine revelation. His visions and dreams guide his family's journey, providing not only direction but also spiritual confirmation and instruction. For modern readers, Lehi's reliance on revelation emphasizes the need for personal and continuous guidance from God in making significant life decisions.

Leadership in Family and Faith

As a patriarch, Lehi's role in leading his family through physical and spiritual wildernesses is instructive. He exemplifies the role of a parent in teaching and nurturing faith within the family unit.

His teachings in 2 Nephi 1-4, where he blesses and counsels his children, highlight the importance of parental involvement in spiritual education and the transmission of religious values.

Enduring Faith Amidst Adversity

Throughout his journey, Lehi faces both external challenges, such as the harsh conditions of the wilderness, and internal challenges, including the murmuring and disobedience of his sons Laman and Lemuel. His patient endurance and continued faithfulness serve as a model for handling life's trials with grace and faith.

The Doctrine of Opposition and Choice

Lehi's teachings on the necessity of opposition and the freedom to choose between good and evil (2 Nephi 2) provide profound doctrinal insights into the purposes of earthly life and the principles of agency and accountability.

In sum, Lehi's narrative is a rich tapestry of prophetic wisdom, exemplifying how to live a Christ-centered life marked by vision, obedience, and resilience. His life is a testament to the transformative power of faith and the eternal principle that individuals must choose to follow Christ to receive the fullness of His blessings.

Sariah: A Pillar of Faith and Devotion

Sariah, the wife of the prophet Lehi and mother to their sons **(1 Nephi 2:5)**, embodies several Christlike attributes that are crucial to her family's spiritual journey and survival. Her faith, though tested, remains a central pillar of her character. While Lehi's faith led the family into the wilderness, it was Sariah's unwavering support that held them together, even in the face of profound uncertainty. She was the resilient matriarch whose unwavering faith and devotion sustained her family through unprecedented trials. Throughout the challenges of leaving Jerusalem and traveling in the wilderness, Sariah sustains her family not only physically but spiritually.

Her resilience and steadfastness shine particularly during times of extreme distress, such as when she fears for the lives of her sons who return to Jerusalem to obtain the brass plates (1 Nephi 5:1-3). Despite her initial despair, her faith is reaffirmed when her sons safely return, leading her to boldly testify, "Now I know of a surety that the Lord hath commanded my husband to flee into the wilderness; yea, and I also know of a surety that the Lord hath protected my sons and delivered them out of the hands of Laban, and given them power whereby they could accomplish the thing which the Lord hath commanded them" (1 Nephi 5:8). This declaration highlights her ability to recognize and affirm the workings of God's hand in her family's life, reflecting a deep-rooted faith and understanding.

Additionally, Sariah's nurturing nature and her role as a caretaker underscore her embodiment of Christlike love and compassion. Her concerns are always for the welfare and safety of her family, reflecting the nurturing aspects of Christ's love.

Lessons and Teachings from Sariah's Life

Sariah's story, though not as extensively documented as those of her husband or sons, provides profound lessons in faith, resilience, and the power of testimony. Her experiences teach us about the strength found in faithfulness, even when the evidence of hope is not visible. Her initial fear and subsequent rejoicing upon her sons' safe return from Jerusalem offer a powerful lesson on trusting God's promises and timing, even in moments of deep personal doubt and fear.

Her role also highlights the crucial support system that family provides in the pursuit of divine commands. Sariah's ability to push forward, despite the uncertainties of wilderness travel and the challenges of uprooting her family from their comfortable life, underscores the sacrifices involved in true discipleship and following God's will.

Moreover, Sariah's life is a testament to the strength and influence of women in sustaining faith and nurturing future generations under challenging circumstances. Her example serves as a reminder of the quiet, often overlooked acts of service and faith that are vital to the Lord's work.

In sum, reflecting on Sariah's character and her journey invites us to consider our own responses to divine directives and personal trials. Her story encourages a recommitment to faith, the importance of family unity, and the nurturing roles we play within our own families and communities. Sariah, like many unsung heroes of the scriptures, offers a model of quiet strength and enduring faith amidst life's storms.

Nephi: A Testament of Faith and Leadership

Nephi, the son of Lehi **(1 Nephi and 2 Nephi)**, is often celebrated as a paragon of obedience, faith, and diligence in the Book of Mormon. His Christlike attributes are evident from the outset of his scriptural journey. When his father, Lehi, receives a divine command to leave Jerusalem, Nephi's response highlights his foundational attribute of faith: "I will go and do the things which the Lord hath commanded" (1 Nephi 3:7). This statement encapsulates his unwavering readiness to obey God's will, setting a pattern for his actions throughout his life. He was a paragon of faith and visionary leadership whose actions shaped the spiritual and temporal course of his people.

Nephi's humility is also notable. Despite his prophetic call and spiritual privileges, he frequently acknowledges his weaknesses and his dependence on divine grace. In a moment of profound self-reflection, he admits, "O wretched man that I am!" (2 Nephi 4:17), echoing the kind of humility that leads to spiritual growth and reliance on the Lord.

Furthermore, Nephi exhibits immense courage and leadership, particularly in his interactions with his rebellious brothers, Laman and Lemuel. His ability to forgive them repeatedly and his efforts to teach and lead them demonstrate his Christlike love and patience.

Lessons and Teachings from Nephi's Life

Nephi's life offers rich lessons in faith and leadership under trial. One of the most significant teachings we can draw from Nephi's experiences is the power of scripture in personal conversion and guidance. Nephi's efforts to obtain the brass plates from Laban in Jerusalem (1 Nephi 4) underscore the importance of scripture as a source of doctrine, law, and history essential for guiding his people according to God's commandments.

Nephi's role as a visionary is marked notably by his profound spiritual experiences, which include his detailed vision of the Tree of Life (1 Nephi 8 & 11). This vision not only confirms the revelations seen by his father but also expands on them, offering Nephi insights into the coming of Jesus Christ, the fate of his descendants, and the eternal nature of God's plan for humanity. His recounting of the vision illustrates the importance of personal revelation in understanding and teaching divine truths.

Perhaps the most enduring lesson from Nephi's life is his constant advocacy for faith and perseverance against adversity. Whether facing physical challenges or spiritual conflicts, Nephi's narrative is a testament to trusting in the Lord's timing and power (1 Nephi 7:12; 18:3). His ability to maintain faith, even when faced with murmuring from his family or personal doubts, provides a powerful blueprint for enduring faith in trials.

Additionally, Nephi teaches us about the nature of true leadership. His leadership style is characterized by service and sacrifice—principles embodied by Jesus Christ. Nephi's construction of the ship, as directed by the Lord (1 Nephi 18), serves as a metaphor for building our lives on a foundation of revelation and obedience.

Nephi's great respect for the prophet Isaiah is evident as he includes many of Isaiah's writings in his record (1 Nephi 20-21; 2 Nephi 12-24). He uses these teachings to underscore the Messiah's coming and the redemption of Israel. Nephi's focus on Isaiah not only reaffirms his own prophecies but also demonstrates the continuity of God's work across different dispensations, emphasizing the importance of scripture in confirming and expanding our understanding of divine purposes.

The doctrine of Jesus Christ, which Nephi expounds in 2 Nephi 31, provides a comprehensive view of the path to eternal life, emphasizing faith in Jesus Christ, repentance, baptism, receiving the Holy Ghost, and enduring to the end. Nephi's teachings encapsulate the core of the gospel, offering a clear blueprint for following Jesus Christ.

In sum, Nephi's journey from Jerusalem to the New World is more than a tale of physical travel; it is a spiritual journey of growth, revelation, and leadership. His life offers profound lessons on the importance of visionary leadership, obedience to God's commandments, the value of scriptures, and the power of enduring faith. Nephi's experiences and teachings continue to inspire and instruct, making his story a cornerstone of spiritual learning and leadership in the Book of Mormon.

Sam: A Model of Support and Steadfastness

Sam, the third son of Lehi and a brother to Nephi, Laman, and Lemuel **(1 Nephi 2:5-6)**, exemplifies several Christlike attributes that underscore his role as a supportive and steadfast figure within the narrative of the Book of Mormon. Unlike his brothers Laman and Lemuel, who frequently exhibit doubt and rebellion, Sam consistently shows faithfulness and loyalty, particularly in supporting Nephi in their many trials.

One of Sam's key attributes is his unwavering faith. He believes in the revelations Nephi receives from God and supports him throughout their journey, including the arduous task of obtaining the brass plates and building a ship to journey to the promised land. His ability to trust in God's guidance and in his brother's prophetic leadership reflects a profound spiritual commitment and resilience.

Additionally, Sam exhibits quiet strength and humility. He does not seek leadership or acknowledgment but instead serves his family and fulfills his duties with diligence and sincerity. This humility is akin to that of Jesus Christ, who taught that "whosoever will be chief among you, let him be your servant" (Matthew 20:27).

Lessons and Teachings from Sam's Life

Sam's character and actions provide valuable lessons on the power of support and faith in leadership and divine guidance. His role, though less prominent than that of Nephi, is critical in the family dynamics and the successful fulfillment of their divine mission.

Supportive Loyalty

Sam's loyalty to Nephi and his alignment with righteous leadership teach us about the importance of support within family and community contexts. His example shows that support need not always be vocal or upfront; it can be quiet yet steadfast and just as impactful. Sam's role encourages us to consider how we support righteous leadership and initiatives within our circles.

Faith in Adversity

Sam's journey is marked by trials, from the threats in Jerusalem to the challenges in the wilderness. His faith through these adversities, particularly his trust in Nephi's visions and leadership, underscores the importance of faith when faced with doubts and fears. This teaches us that steadfast faith can help us endure challenges and contribute to collective goals, even when the end is not clearly in sight.

Humility in Service

Sam's humility, evidenced by his contentment in playing a supportive role and his lack of contention for leadership, highlights the strength in humility and service. This mirrors Christ's teachings on leadership and service, emphasizing that true greatness often lies in being a humble servant.

In sum, Sam's life is an exemplary model of supportive loyalty, steadfast faith, and humble service. His contributions, though subtle, are significant, illustrating that every member within a community or family has an important role, regardless of whether it is in the limelight. His story teaches us that our quiet, consistent support and faith can make a profound difference in achieving collective spiritual and temporal goals.

Jacob: A Prophet of Justice and Redemption

Jacob, the brother of Nephi and a prominent figure in the Book of Mormon **(2 Nephi 2:1-30; Jacob 1-7)**, is known for his deep spirituality, doctrinal insights, and profound empathy. From an early age, Jacob suffered afflictions yet showed a remarkable devotion to God's teachings, which Nephi attributed to the tender mercies of the Lord (2 Nephi 2:1). Jacob's Christlike attributes include his commitment to truth, his fervent preaching against materialism and inequality, and his emphasis on the Atonement of Jesus Christ as central to salvation. He was a prophet born in the wilderness, known for his unyielding teachings on justice, mercy, and the necessity of spiritual rebirth.

Lessons and Teachings from Jacob's Life and Writings

Jacob's contributions to Nephite society and his doctrinal expositions in the Book of Mormon provide valuable lessons on ethical leadership, spiritual diligence, and the redemptive power of faith in Christ.

The Balancing Act of Justice and Mercy

In his sermons, Jacob often tackles complex issues of justice and mercy, reflecting a profound understanding of their interplay in the divine plan. In Jacob 2-3, he addresses the people with sharp rebukes against pride and immorality but also offers hope and mercy to those who repent. His approach teaches us about the necessity of maintaining justice in society while always allowing room for mercy and redemption. This dual focus challenges us to apply the same principles in our dealings, promoting fairness while offering compassion and support for rehabilitation.

The Importance of True Doctrine

Jacob's teachings are heavily doctrinal, particularly emphasizing the Atonement of Jesus Christ and the plan of salvation (2 Nephi 9). He clarifies and expounds these doctrines with the intent to fortify the faith of his people and guide them towards spiritual freedom. From Jacob's example, we learn the importance of grounding our spiritual lives in sound doctrine, ensuring that our beliefs and practices align with divine truths, which serve as a foundation for moral and ethical living.

Confronting Materialism and Social Inequality

Jacob's bold condemnation of wealth disparity and his admonitions against the pursuit of riches demonstrate his concern for social equality and spiritual wellness (Jacob 2:13-21). His warnings against materialism are profoundly relevant today, reminding us of the dangers of allowing wealth and status to dictate our values and interactions. His teachings encourage us to foster societies where compassion and communal welfare predominate over individual gain.

Enduring Faith Amidst Trials

Despite the early hardships and ongoing challenges he faced, Jacob's life is a testament to enduring faith. His perseverance in teaching, leading, and nurturing his people, even in the face of personal and communal trials, exemplifies the strength that comes from a deep and abiding faith in God. His example inspires us to remain steadfast in our convictions and diligent in our spiritual commitments, regardless of the adversities we encounter.

In sum, Jacob's life and teachings in the Book of Mormon offer profound insights into leading a life dedicated to spiritual principles, doctrinal integrity, and social justice. His legacy is a powerful reminder of the impact that one devoted individual can have on their community and future generations, challenging us to live with purpose, dedication, and an unwavering commitment to divine principles.

Joseph: A Legacy of Promise and Prophecy

Joseph, the youngest son of Lehi in the Book of Mormon **(2 Nephi 3:1-25)**, stands out for his receptivity to spiritual blessings and the significant prophecies pronounced upon him by his father. Although specific details about his actions are sparse, the blessings and prophecies indicate that Joseph was seen as faithful and worthy of carrying forward a divine legacy. His character is marked by an evident willingness to adhere to his father's teachings and to embrace his role in the unfolding narrative of his people, reflecting Christlike attributes of humility and faith.

Lessons and Teachings from Joseph's Life and Blessings

Joseph's life, though not elaborately detailed in the Book of Mormon, is rich with lessons derived from the prophetic blessings he received from his father, Lehi, which intertwine with Joseph of Egypt's prophecies about a seer named Joseph who would come in the latter days.

Heritage and Prophecy

Lehi's blessing to Joseph emphasizes the covenants made with their forefathers, connecting Joseph to the ancient patriarch Joseph of Egypt. This lineage and the associated prophecies (2 Nephi 3) underscore the importance of understanding and appreciating one's heritage. For modern readers, this teaches the value of recognizing and embracing one's spiritual and familial legacies as guiding forces in life. It invites reflection on how we honor and carry forward the legacies and teachings from our ancestors.

The Role of Seers and Revelators

In his prophecies, Lehi speaks of a future seer named Joseph, linking his son to Joseph Smith, who would play a pivotal role in the restoration of the gospel. This prophecy highlights the crucial roles that seers and revelators hold in the unfolding plan of God. Reflecting on this, we can appreciate the continuity of God's work through chosen individuals across dispensations and learn to trust in and follow the guidance of modern prophets and revelators more deeply.

Faith and Destiny

Joseph's story also teaches about the interplay between divine destiny and personal faith. Despite being younger and perhaps less prominently featured than his brothers, Joseph is assured a significant spiritual legacy, showing that individual roles in God's plan are not always tied to prominence or conventional success. This lesson encourages a personal reflection on how we view and accept our roles within God's larger plan, fostering faith that God equips and uses each person uniquely for His purposes.

Continuity of Divine Promises

Lastly, the blessings upon Joseph illustrate the continuity and fulfillment of God's promises over generations. The specific promises to Joseph echo through centuries, culminating in significant events in scriptural history. This teaches us about the reliability and eternal nature of God's words and promises. Reflecting on this, we are reminded to trust in God's promises and timing, maintaining faith that His purposes will be accomplished, even if not on our immediate timeline.

In sum, Joseph's character and the prophecies about him in the Book of Mormon offer profound insights into the themes of divine legacy, prophetic guidance, personal faith, and the fulfillment of God's promises. His life encourages us to embrace our roles in God's plan with humility and faith, trusting in the continuity and fulfillment of divine promises through our lives and beyond.

Daughters of Lehi: Silent Pillars of Strength and Faith

The daughters of Lehi, mentioned briefly in the Book of Mormon **(2 Nephi 5:6)**, epitomize the Christlike attributes of steadfastness, resilience, and support. While the scriptures provide limited details about their individual actions, their role within Lehi's family during the formidable journey from Jerusalem to the Americas and in establishing a new settlement suggests significant inner strength and commitment to their family's divine mission. These women likely embodied a quiet but profound support system, upholding their family, both spiritually and physically, throughout their trials.

Lessons and Teachings from the Life of the Daughters of Lehi

Strength in Silence and Support

The daughters of Lehi, while not prominently featured in scriptural narratives, play crucial supportive roles in the background. Their presence during the family's journey and settlement speaks to the vital role often played quietly by many who support their families in times of change and challenge. This teaches us the value of every member's contribution, regardless of whether it is loudly celebrated or quietly executed. Reflecting on this, we might consider the often-overlooked contributions in our own lives and communities. How do we recognize and value the silent yet strong support provided by others?

Resilience in the Face of Adversity

The very act of enduring a journey fraught with unknowns and establishing a new life in a foreign land highlights remarkable resilience. The daughters of Lehi's ability to persevere through physical hardships and psychological challenges underscores a resilience that is deeply Christlike. This resilience invites us to reflect on our own responses to adversity. Are we equipped with a faith and fortitude that sustain us through trials? How do we cultivate such resilience in ourselves and encourage it in others?

Faith and Commitment to Divine Directives

The daughters of Lehi's journey with their family are fundamentally a journey of faith, driven by their father's prophetic visions and commandments from God. Their commitment to this faith-driven journey, despite the uncertainties and sacrifices involved, teaches us about the depth of faith required to follow divine directives. This prompts us to assess our own commitment to our beliefs and directives we feel are inspired. How deep does our faith go when called to leave behind the familiar for the unknown?

Building Foundations for Future Generations

The daughters of Lehi were part of laying the foundational stones of what would become the Nephite civilization. Their role, likely encompassing both participation in establishing societal norms and in raising the next generation, highlights the importance of building strong foundations for future communities. Reflecting on this, we can consider how our actions today are contributing to the foundations of our future communities. What kind of legacy are we helping to build?

In sum, although the scriptural account provides only glimpses into the lives of Lehi's daughters, their story enriches our understanding of the vital roles played by those who may not stand in the spotlight but whose strength, faith, and resilience are crucial to the success of collective endeavors. Their example challenges us to appreciate and emulate the quiet yet powerful attributes of steadfast support, resilient faith, and foundational commitment in our own lives.

Author's Reflection

Reflecting on the lives of Lehi, Sariah, Nephi, Sam, Jacob, Joseph, and the daughters of Lehi, I am struck by how their collective journey from Jerusalem to the promised land is not just a physical exodus but a profound spiritual pilgrimage. Each character contributes uniquely to the foundation of faith that underpins the Nephite civilization, offering timeless lessons that resonate with our modern personal and communal lives.

Lehi: Prophet and Patriarch

Lehi's unwavering faith in divine revelation is foundational. Lehi's immediate obedience to the Lord's command (1 Nephi 2:2-4) exemplifies his profound trust in God's plan, showing that true spiritual receptivity involves not just hearing divine guidance but acting on it without hesitation. This readiness is a hallmark of those who are spiritually prepared to lead others toward their promised lands. Lehi's visions and prophetic insights (1 Nephi 1:8, 1 Nephi 5:4) not only guide his family but also lay the groundwork for their spiritual and physical journey to the promised land. His life teaches us the importance of seeking and trusting in personal revelation, even when the path is fraught with uncertainty.

In modern times, Lehi's example challenges us to heed divine promptings, especially when they require significant sacrifice. Just as Lehi's faith led his family to a new land of promise, our faith can lead us to personal and communal "promised lands"—places of spiritual growth, peace, and fulfillment. In moments of decision, we must ask ourselves: Are we, like Lehi, willing to leave our "Jerusalem"—our comfort zones—for the unknown, trusting that God's promises will be fulfilled?

Sariah: A Pillar of Faith and Devotion

Sariah's journey from doubt to firm testimony (1 Nephi 5:8) is a powerful narrative of spiritual resilience. Initially, she struggles with fear and uncertainty as her sons return to Jerusalem for the brass plates. Her worry is not just maternal but deeply human, reflecting the anxieties we all face when loved ones are at risk. Yet, Sariah's faith is ultimately strengthened through her experiences, leading her to testify to the Lord's protection and the divine nature of their mission.

For us today, Sariah represents the strength that comes from faith, especially in times of trial. Her story reminds us that doubt is a natural part of the faith journey, but it is through persistence in faith that we find divine reassurance. In our modern lives, Sariah's example calls us to support our families and communities with *unwavering faith, trusting in God's promises even when the outcomes are uncertain.*

Nephi: A Testament of Faith and Leadership

Nephi's declaration, "I will go and do the things which the Lord hath commanded" (1 Nephi 3:7), encapsulates his defining characteristic: proactive faith. Nephi's leadership, grounded in his firm testimony of Christ (2 Nephi 25:26), not only drives his family forward but also exemplifies modern leadership principles—where true leaders inspire others to rise to their potential through example and unwavering commitment to righteous principles. His ability to motivate and lead by example teaches us that true leadership ignites faith and action in others. His construction of the ship (1 Nephi 17:8-9) symbolizes his ability to turn divine instructions into tangible actions, a principle that is crucial for any spiritual or communal endeavor.

In today's world, Nephi's example is a call to action. It is not enough to simply believe; we must translate our faith into works (James 2:17). Whether we are leading our families, communities, or personal lives, Nephi's life urges us to take bold steps toward our "promised lands," knowing that divine guidance will illuminate our path. As we face our own challenges, we might ask ourselves: Are we, like Nephi, willing to take bold steps toward our goals, trusting in the guidance we receive? Nephi teaches us that faith and leadership are inseparable; true leadership is grounded in a deep commitment to God's will.

Sam: A Model of Support and Steadfastness

Sam, often overshadowed by his more prominent brothers, exhibits a quiet but steadfast faith. His loyalty to Nephi and his consistent support (1 Nephi 2:17) demonstrate that faithfulness does not always seek the spotlight. Sam's role, though less celebrated, is crucial in maintaining the unity and morale of the group. His willingness to follow Nephi without contention reflects humility and dedication that are essential in any collective journey.

Sam's example speaks to the importance of supportive roles in our personal and communal lives today. Not everyone is called to lead, but everyone's contribution is vital. In our communities, we must recognize and value the "Sams" among us—those who support, sustain, and strengthen the fabric of our shared endeavors. Sam's life reminds us that steadfast support and humble service are as crucial to achieving our goals as bold leadership.

Jacob: A Prophet of Justice and Redemption

Jacob's life, marked by his teachings on justice, mercy, and the Atonement (2 Nephi 9), reflects his deep understanding of the gospel's core principles. Born in the wilderness, Jacob's experiences with hardship and divine instruction shaped his profound empathy and moral conviction. His sermons on pride, wealth, and social inequality (Jacob 2:13-21) are not just doctrinal but deeply practical, addressing the challenges his people face.

Jacob's teachings are profoundly relevant to modern life, where issues of justice and inequality are ever-present. His emphasis on the Atonement as the means of overcoming sin and division calls us to apply Christ's teachings in our interactions with others, particularly in advocating for the marginalized. Jacob's life challenges us to live with integrity, to champion justice in our communities, and to rely on Christ's redemptive power to heal societal wounds.

Joseph: A Legacy of Promise and Prophecy

Joseph, though mentioned less frequently, carries a significant prophetic legacy (2 Nephi 3). His father's blessings tie him to the ancient Joseph of Egypt and the latter-day prophet Joseph Smith, highlighting the continuity of God's promises across generations. Joseph's life symbolizes the faithfulness required to inherit and fulfill divine prophecies, reminding us that understanding our spiritual heritage can empower us to embrace our roles in God's plan with greater conviction. In a world where immediate results are often expected, Joseph reminds us that true faith involves trusting in divine timing, knowing that our role, *though it may seem small now, contributes to a much larger fulfillment of God's promises.*

For us today, Joseph's example is a reminder of the importance of embracing our spiritual heritage and remaining faithful to the divine promises extended to us. Whether in our personal lives or within our communities, we are all part of a larger divine narrative. Joseph's life calls us to be patient and faithful, trusting that God's promises will be fulfilled in His time, and that our role, though it may seem small, is vital in the unfolding of His greater plan.

Daughters of Lehi: Silent Pillars of Strength and Faith

The daughters of Lehi, though unnamed, are an integral part of their family's journey. Their silent resilience (2 Nephi 5:6) serves as a powerful testament to the essential role women play in sustaining faith and family—roles often unrecognized yet deeply influential. Just as these daughters of Lehi quietly upheld the family, many women today continue to be the unseen pillars that hold families and communities together. Their quiet strength and commitment reflect the deep-rooted faith that holds the community together in times of trial.

In modern contexts, the daughters of Lehi remind us of the crucial roles women play in our families and communities. Their example calls us to recognize and honor the contributions of those who, like them, work behind the scenes to ensure the success and well-being of the collective. Their faith and resilience are a powerful testament to the sustaining power of women's influence in both spiritual and temporal matters.

Summary

The foundation of faith laid by these early figures is not merely a historical account; it is a living blueprint for how we can build our own spiritual and communal lives today. As we reflect on their examples, we are invited to apply these timeless lessons in our own journeys, ensuring that our paths, like theirs, lead us to our promised lands. Lehi, Sariah, Nephi, Sam, Jacob, Joseph, and the daughters of Lehi each contribute unique insights into the nature of faith, leadership, support, justice, prophecy, and resilience. Their lives challenge us to build our own "promised lands"—whether they are spiritual, familial, or communal—on the firm foundation of faith, divine guidance, and collective strength.

As I reflect on these early saints, I am reminded that their ancient principles are not relics of the past but living guidelines that continue to apply to our lives today. Their examples inspire us to lead with faith, support with humility, and act with justice, trusting in the promises of God. It inspires me to lead with faith, support with humility, act with justice, and trust in the promises of God. Just as these early saints forged a path to their promised land, we too are on a journey, guided by the same divine principles that brought them to their destination.

Chapter 2

Reluctant Followers and Adversaries

Lehi's journey from Jerusalem to the promised land was fraught with opposition, both from within his family and from external adversaries. The struggles presented by Laban, Laman, Lemuel, and Sherem served as critical tests of faith and obedience, offering profound lessons on the complexities of following divine guidance. In examining the lives of Laban, Laman, Lemuel, and Sherem figures who opposed the prophetic mission and leadership of Lehi and Nephi we gain a deeper understanding of the adversities faced by these early pioneers of faith. The historical context in which these challenges arose is crucial to appreciating the full impact of their stories. Understanding their roles provides a deeper perspective on the adversities faced and the enduring lessons of faith and perseverance.

Historical Context

Lehi's prophetic mission and his family's exodus from Jerusalem unfolded during a period of profound spiritual and political turmoil. Jerusalem, teetering on the brink of destruction, was a city where righteousness clashed with widespread corruption, making the divine command to leave all the more urgent and challenging. Jerusalem, around 600 BC, was a city rife with corruption and impending doom, as prophesied by many, including Jeremiah. Against this backdrop, God called Lehi to lead his family into the wilderness to preserve a righteous branch of Israel (1 Nephi 1:4).

Characters in Chapter 2

- **Laban** ~ A Jerusalem leader whose possession of the brass plates posed a significant obstacle, ultimately leading to a confrontation that tested the boundaries of divine command and moral action.
- **Laman** ~ The eldest son of Lehi, whose frequent opposition and struggle with faith led to familial divisions and significant lessons in the consequences of rebellion.
- **Lemuel** ~ The second son of Lehi, often following in Laman's footsteps, whose lack of personal conviction highlights the dangers of succumbing to external influences.

- **Sherem** ~ An articulate skeptic who confronted Jacob, challenging the Nephite's foundational beliefs in Christ, and whose story underscores the perils of intellectual pride and the necessity of humility.

Understanding these figures and their opposition provides crucial insights into the dynamics of faith, obedience, and conflict. Their interactions with Lehi, Nephi, and other faithful members of the group offer timeless lessons on the importance of steadfastness in the face of adversity, the consequences of rebellion, and the enduring power of divine guidance.

Laban: A Complex Figure in Nephite Narrative

Laban, a leader in Jerusalem from whom Nephi obtains the brass plates **(1 Nephi 3:2-3)**, is predominantly portrayed as a figure of opposition in the Book of Mormon. His role, as seen through the narrative lens of Nephi, contrasts sharply with Christlike virtues, primarily serving as a counterexample of how power and authority can be misused. Laban is described as a wealthy and influential man, having command over a garrison and possession of sacred records crucial to Lehi's family. However, his refusal to part with the brass plates, coupled with his willingness to threaten the lives of Lehi's sons, highlights attributes of greed, ruthlessness, and unrighteous dominion.

Lessons and Teachings from Laban's Story

What can we learn from Laban's interactions with Nephi and his brothers? His story offers profound insights into the themes of justice, the use of power, and divine providence.

Misuse of Authority and Power

Laban's refusal to give up the brass plates, even at the cost of threatening murder, is a stark illustration of the misuse of power. His actions serve as a vital lesson in the dangers of authority when it is not tempered by righteousness. For those in positions of power,

Laban's example is a cautionary tale about the ethical responsibilities that come with leadership. It encourages a reflection on how we, in any position of influence, wield our power—whether in accordance with moral principles or driven by personal gain.

Divine Providence and Moral Challenges

The most critical part of Laban's narrative is Nephi's commanded slaying of Laban to obtain the brass plates after Laban's repeated refusals and assaults (1 Nephi 4:5-18). This incident raises complex questions about morality, obedience, and the workings of divine providence. It teaches that sometimes, divine purposes may involve difficult and morally challenging actions, but also emphasizes the need for seeking and following divine guidance in such moments. The story compels us to consider how far we are willing to go in obedience to divine commands and the importance of clear, confirmed guidance in such circumstances.

Justice and Consequences

Laban's fate also speaks to a broader principle of scriptural justice—" that which ye sow, so shall ye reap" (Galatians 6:7). His own sword, the instrument he likely used to threaten Nephi and his brothers, is ultimately used against him. This ironic twist underscores the scriptural theme that unrighteous deeds eventually bring about one's downfall.

In sum, while Laban is not a model of Christlike attributes, his role in the Book of Mormon provides essential lessons about the moral complexities of life's challenges, the responsibilities that accompany power, and the intricate ways in which divine purposes unfold. Reflecting on Laban's story encourages a deeper examination of our actions, motivations, and the ethical dilemmas we may face, urging a steadfast adherence to righteousness, especially when faced with difficult decisions. While Laban's story warns of the dangers of power, Laman's life illustrates the internal struggle with faith that can lead even the most favored of God's children astray.

Laman: A Study in Struggle and Lessons in Agency

Laman, as the eldest son of Lehi **(1 Nephi 2:5)**, occupies a complex position within the narrative of the Book of Mormon. While not typically noted for Christlike attributes in the way his brother Nephi is, Laman's story offers a nuanced view of human nature and the struggle between obedience and rebellion. His character reflects the challenges that many face in exercising faith and obedience, particularly when faced with uncertainty or adversity.

Though often depicted negatively due to his murmuring and disobedience, there are moments that suggest a potential for leadership and concern for his family, albeit overshadowed by his doubts and fears. For example, his initial reluctance to leave Jerusalem could be seen as a concern for the welfare and security of his family, reflecting a very human apprehension towards drastic life changes (1 Nephi 2:11-12).

Lessons and Teachings from Laman's Life

Laman's life offers critical insights into the nature of agency, the consequences of rebellion, and the complexities of family and faith dynamics. His story is a cautionary tale that invites reflection on the importance of faith, the dangers of hard-heartedness, and the profound impact of our choices.

Struggle with Faith and Obedience

Throughout the narrative, Laman exhibits a recurring struggle to exercise faith and obedience. His skepticism and occasional outright rebellion against the commands received by his father from God highlight a universal human challenge—trusting divine guidance over our understanding and fears. This struggle is particularly evident in his and his brother Lemuel's repeated murmurings during their wilderness journey and their attempts to return to Jerusalem (1 Nephi 3:31).

Consequences of Rebellion

Laman's actions provide a vivid illustration of the consequences of rebellion against God's commandments. His repeated decisions to go against divine instructions lead not only to personal strife but also to familial discord. This discord sows seeds of enmity that affect generations, illustrating the long-term consequences of our choices, not just for ourselves but for our posterity (2 Nephi 5:6).

Opportunities for Repentance and Redemption

Despite his faults, Laman is repeatedly given opportunities to repent and change, which underscores a fundamental gospel principle of love and redemption. Each instance where he chooses temporarily to align with his family's goals under Nephi's leadership, although short-lived, shows that change is always a possibility, regardless of past failures (1 Nephi 7:21).

In sum, Laman's life teaches us about the importance of choosing faith over doubt and obedience over rebellion. It reminds us that while moral agency allows us to make our choices, it also binds us to the consequences of those choices. Reflecting on Laman's life encourages us to examine our faith, our responses to divine commandments, and our interactions with those whom our decisions affect. It is a solemn reminder that while redemption is always within reach, our choices significantly shape our spiritual journey and relationships.

Lemuel: A Study in Influence and Choice

Lemuel, the second son of Lehi **(1 Nephi 2:5)**, often appears in the narrative shadowed by his older brother Laman in the Book of Mormon. His character, though less prominently detailed than those of his brothers Laman and Nephi, presents a compelling study of the influences of familial ties and peer pressure. Christlike attributes are less often directly attributed to Lemuel, but a deeper look into his actions and the context in which he lived reveals the complexities of his spiritual journey.

Lemuel displays loyalty, albeit misdirected at times towards his brother Laman rather than a righteous cause. This can be seen as a form of faithfulness, albeit skewed by his allegiance to his brother's dissent rather than to his father's prophetic guidance. His life serves as a reflective mirror for examining how one's environment and close relationships can significantly sway one's decisions and moral compass.

Lessons and Teachings from Lemuel's Life

Lemuel's character and the narrative arc that encompasses his actions provide foundational lessons about the influence of companionship and the significance of personal conviction.

Influence and Companionship

Lemuel's tendency to align with Laman, often participating in murmuring against their father's directives (1 Nephi 2:11-12), underscores how significant others' influences can be in one's life. This aspect of his character invites reflection on the sources of influence in our own lives. Are our actions and beliefs genuinely our own, or are they unduly shaped by those around us? Lemuel teaches us the importance of scrutinizing the motivations behind our allegiances and the potential consequences of following without personal conviction.

Lack of Personal Conviction

Lemuel often lacks a personal testimony of the visions and instructions that guide his family's journey. This absence of personal conviction makes him susceptible to doubt and fear, illustrating the peril of relying solely on the faith and experiences of others rather than developing one's own. The lesson here is clear: personal conviction is crucial in sustaining faith through challenges and changes. Without it, one's spiritual foundation remains vulnerable to external pressures and internal uncertainties.

Consequences of Choices

Throughout the narrative, Lemuel faces various consequences due to his choices, from angelic reprimands to familial strife (1 Nephi 3:28-29). These episodes highlight that our choices, especially when made without firm personal convictions, can lead not only to personal regrets but also to broader impacts on those around us. Lemuel's life serves as a cautionary tale about the importance of making informed, personally convicted decisions that align with divine will rather than mere human influence.

In sum, reflecting on Lemuel's life and actions encourages a deeper examination of our influences, convictions, and the choices we make in response to God's commands. His story serves as a poignant reminder of the need for personal faith development and the careful consideration of whose influence we allow to steer our actions and decisions.

Sherem: Skepticism and the Consequences of Demanding Signs

Sherem, as depicted in the Book of Mormon **(Jacob 7:1-20)**, serves as a notable example of what happens when intellectual pride and skepticism overshadow humility and faith. While not embodying Christlike attributes directly, Sherem's story is instructive as it highlights the dangers of a hardened heart and a closed mind. Sherem is articulate, confident, and skilled in rhetoric, using these talents not to uplift or edify but to challenge and deceive. His demand for a sign from God, rather than seeking understanding through faith, reflects a reliance on physical proof over spiritual conviction, illustrating the pitfalls of relying solely on empirical evidence in matters of faith.

Lessons and Teachings from Sherem's Confrontation with Jacob

Sherem's encounter with Jacob offers several key lessons about faith, the nature of true signs, and the importance of humility in spiritual matters.

The Dangers of Intellectual Pride

Sherem's argument against Jesus Christ's divinity and the Atonement reveals a man led by intellectual pride rather than genuine inquiry. His approach serves as a cautionary tale about the limits of human reasoning in divine matters. Sherem's reliance on his intellectual capabilities and his manipulation of rhetoric demonstrate that knowledge, without humility and openness to divine truth, can lead to spiritual downfall. This scenario invites us to examine our own approaches to spiritual knowledge: Do we seek to understand, or do we seek to disprove?

The Role of Signs in Faith

Sherem's demand for a sign from Jacob reflects a misunderstanding of the purpose and place of divine signs. In religious contexts, signs are often meant to confirm faith, not to initiate it. Sherem's insistence on a sign and the devastating consequences that follow when he receives it underscore that true faith must precede divine confirmation. This lesson is crucial in understanding that while signs from God can strengthen faith, they should not be the foundation of it. It challenges us to build our faith on the teachings of the scriptures and the whisperings of the Holy Spirit.

Humility and Repentance

The end of Sherem's story is marked by his public confession of Jesus Christ and acknowledgment of his mistakes. This act of humility, though coming late, highlights the power of repentance and the possibility of forgiveness. Sherem's repentance serves as a poignant reminder of the redemptive power of humility and the importance of keeping our hearts open to the truths God seeks to teach us. It teaches us the importance of admitting our errors and realigning ourselves with God's will when we have strayed.

In sum, Sherem's narrative in the Book of Mormon, while serving as a warning, also provides deep insights into the dynamics of faith, the dangers of skepticism unrestrained by humility, and the merciful nature of God's justice. Through his story, we learn about the essential balance between reason and faith, the proper role of divine signs, and the enduring possibility of redemption through repentance. His story enriches our understanding of these principles and invites us to apply them thoughtfully in our own spiritual journeys.

Author's Reflection

Reflecting on the lives of Laban, Laman, Lemuel, and Sherem, I am struck by the complex interplay of faith, agency, and rebellion. These characters, though often seen as antagonists, provide crucial lessons about the consequences of our choices, the nature of doubt and disbelief, and the ever-present opportunity for repentance. Their stories are not merely cautionary tales but are rich with insights that apply to our modern personal and communal journeys toward our own promised lands.

Laban: The Misuse of Power and Its Consequences

Laban, a man of wealth and authority in Jerusalem, represents the dangers of misusing power and the inevitable consequences that follow. His refusal to part with the brass plates, despite knowing their spiritual significance to Lehi's family, demonstrates a profound moral failure. Laban's actions, as recounted in 1 Nephi 3:13 and 1 Nephi 4:22, are emblematic of a broader spiritual decline in Jerusalem—where material wealth and power became the gods that people served, overshadowing the eternal principles of righteousness and integrity.

Reflecting on Laban's life, I see a stark warning about the dangers of allowing worldly power to corrupt our judgment and integrity. His story challenges all who hold positions of influence to lead with righteousness, remembering that true power lies in service and humility rather than in domination and control. In modern life, Laban's story challenges us to examine how we use the influence and resources at our disposal. Are we using our positions to serve others and further God's purposes, or are we clinging to power for personal gain? Laban's tragic end, where his own sword is used against him (1 Nephi 4:18), serves as a stark reminder that the misuse of power is a path to inevitable downfall, both spiritually and temporally. This lesson is particularly poignant for modern leaders, who must navigate the fine line between authority and ethical responsibility.

Laman: The Struggle Between Faith and Doubt

Laman, the eldest son of Lehi, is a complex figure whose life is marked by a constant struggle between faith and doubt. His initial reluctance to leave Jerusalem and his frequent complaints during the journey (1 Nephi 2:11-12) reflect a deep-seated fear of the unknown and a lack of trust in divine guidance. Despite witnessing miraculous events, such as the appearance of an angel (1 Nephi 3:29), Laman's faith remains shaky, leading him to repeatedly rebel against his father and brother Nephi.

Laman's story resonates deeply with the modern struggle to maintain faith amidst uncertainty and adversity. How often do we find ourselves in Laman's shoes, grappling with doubt and fear in the face of the unknown? It challenges us to examine our own reactions to divine guidance—do we, like Laman, allow doubt and fear to dominate, or do we choose to trust in God's plan, even when it defies our understanding? His life teaches us that faith is not simply about believing in God's power but about trusting His plan, even when it defies our understanding. In our personal and communal lives, Laman's example challenges us to confront our doubts and fears directly, recognizing that these struggles are a natural part of the faith journey. The consequences of Laman's rebellion, which ultimately led to the division of his family (2 Nephi 5:6), remind us that unresolved doubts and persistent disobedience can fracture relationships and derail our progress toward our own promised lands.

Lemuel: The Influence of Companionship and the Need for Personal Conviction

Lemuel, often seen as a follower of his older brother Laman, represents the dangers of allowing others to dictate our beliefs and actions. His consistent alignment with Laman's rebelliousness (1 Nephi 2:13) underscores the powerful influence of companionship on our spiritual journey. Unlike Nephi, who develops a strong personal conviction and relationship with God, Lemuel seems to lack a firm foundation of faith, making him susceptible to external pressures.

Reflecting on Lemuel's life, I am reminded of the importance of cultivating personal conviction and discernment in our spiritual lives. In today's world, where we are constantly influenced by those around us—whether through social media, peer groups, or cultural norms—Lemuel's story serves as a cautionary tale about the dangers of spiritual dependence. Lemuel's story urges us to cultivate our own spiritual foundations, independent of external influences. This is not just an internal task but a daily practice—standing firm in our beliefs, even when those around us waver, and ensuring that our spiritual compass is guided by divine principles rather than by the shifting opinions of others. It prompts us to ask: Are we living our lives based on our convictions and divine guidance, or are we merely following the crowd? Lemuel's inability to break away from Laman's negative influence ultimately leads to his downfall, illustrating that without a strong personal foundation, we are vulnerable to being led astray from our path to the promised land.

Sherem: The Dangers of Intellectual Pride and the Role of Humility in Faith

Sherem, who confronts Jacob with skepticism about Christ's divinity and the Atonement (Jacob 7:6-7), embodies the dangers of intellectual pride and the rejection of spiritual truths. Sherem's reliance on logic and rhetoric, rather than faith and revelation, leads him to demand a sign from God. This pivotal moment in his life reveals the inherent limitations of human understanding when confronted with divine truth, a lesson that echoes through the ages, challenging us to rely on faith rather than solely on empirical evidence. His story challenges us to consider the role of faith as a bridge between what we can understand and what we must trust in God (Jacob 7:13). When that sign is given, it leads to his immediate recognition of his error and subsequent confession (Jacob 7:17).

Sherem's story is particularly relevant in modern times, where skepticism and the demand for empirical evidence often overshadow faith. His life warns us of the limits of human reasoning when it comes to understanding divine principles. In our pursuit of knowledge and truth, Sherem challenges us to maintain humility and openness to spiritual insights that transcend human logic. His ultimate repentance and acknowledgment of Christ (Jacob 7:19) highlight the importance of humility in our spiritual journey. Sherem teaches us that no matter how far we stray, the path to redemption is always open if we are willing to humble ourselves and embrace the truth.

Summary

The characters of Chapter 2—Laban, Laman, Lemuel, and Sherem—each offer unique insights into the complexities of faith, power, influence, and humility. Their lives serve as both warnings and lessons for our modern spiritual and communal journeys.

Laban's misuse of power reminds us to wield our influence with integrity and in service of divine purposes. Laman's struggle with faith and doubt teaches us the importance of trusting God's plan, even in the face of uncertainty. Lemuel's susceptibility to external influences challenges us to develop personal conviction and discernment. Sherem's intellectual pride and eventual repentance highlight the need for humility and the recognition that faith often requires embracing truths beyond human logic. As we reflect on the lives of Laban, Laman, Lemuel, and Sherem, we are reminded that the path to our promised lands is fraught with challenges, both from within and without. These characters teach us to wield our power with integrity, to trust in God's plan despite our doubts, to cultivate personal conviction, and to approach our faith with humility.

As I reflect on these lives, I am reminded that our journey to our own promised lands—whether spiritual, personal, or communal—requires not only careful navigation but also a steadfast commitment to the lessons these figures impart. By embracing their stories, we arm ourselves with the wisdom to face our own challenges, ensuring that we stay true to our divine purpose. By learning from the experiences of Laban, Laman, Lemuel, and Sherem, we prepare ourselves not just to face the trials ahead but to do so with unwavering faith and a deep commitment to our divine path. Their stories serve as both warnings and guideposts, helping us to navigate our own journeys with wisdom, integrity, and humility.

Chapter 3

Allies from Jerusalem

The journey of Lehi's family from Jerusalem to the promised land was shaped not only by their own faith and determination but also by the inclusion of key allies who joined them along the way. This chapter explores the roles of Zoram, Ishmael, Ishmael's wife, and their daughters, who became integral members of Lehi's group, enriching the narrative with their contributions and the dynamics they introduced. Understanding their contributions and the dynamics they introduced provides a richer context for the collaborative efforts that were essential in overcoming the challenges and achieving the successes of the group during their journey.

Historical Context

Around 600 BC, as Jerusalem faced imminent destruction due to widespread wickedness, God commanded Lehi to lead his family into the wilderness (1 Nephi 1:4). This divine directive set them on a path fraught with challenges but also guided by profound revelations and divine assistance. The inclusion of allies from Jerusalem significantly impacted their journey and the establishment of their new society in the promised land.

Characters in Chapter 3

- **Zoram** ~ Once a servant of Laban, Zoram's decision to join Nephi's family symbolizes unwavering loyalty and the power of unity in the face of adversity.
- **Ishmael** ~ A respected elder from Jerusalem, Ishmael's faith led his family to join Lehi's group, exemplifying the strength of community and the importance of shared spiritual purpose.
- **Ishmael's Wife** ~ A pillar of support, Ishmael's wife embodies resilience and quiet strength, providing the emotional foundation necessary for her family's arduous journey.
- **Daughters of Ishmael** ~ Courageous and devoted, the daughters of Ishmael played a crucial role in defending

Nephi and fostering the familial bonds that solidified the unity of Lehi's group.

This historical context highlights the importance of alliances and the integration of diverse individuals in achieving a common divine mission. The roles and contributions of Zoram, Ishmael, Ishmael's wife, and their daughters enrich the narrative of Lehi's journey, emphasizing themes of faith, loyalty, unity, and the essential contributions of both men and women in the fulfillment of God's commandments. Understanding these allies from Jerusalem provides deeper insights into the collaborative and communal aspects of the early Nephite society.

Zoram: A Study in Loyalty and Integration

Zoram, initially Laban's servant (1 Nephi 4:20-35), emerges in the Book of Mormon narrative under extraordinary circumstances. His decision to join Nephi and his family after the slaying of Laban displays several Christlike attributes, notably loyalty and courage. Once Zoram understands Nephi's intentions and the divine guidance behind their actions, he makes a pivotal choice to leave his previous life behind and align himself with Lehi's family. His commitment is solidified through an oath, where Nephi swears unto Zoram that he shall be a free man like unto us if he goes down into the wilderness with us (1 Nephi 4:33). This promise marks the beginning of Zoram's integration into Nephi's group, showcasing his trust and willingness to embrace new faith and community.

Lessons and Teachings from Zoram's Life

Zoram's transition from Laban's servant to a member of Lehi's family offers profound lessons in trust, loyalty, and the embracing of new beginnings.

Trust and Loyalty

Zoram's decision to trust Nephi and join Lehi's family, especially after such a dramatic and life-altering confrontation, underscores his capacity for trust and adaptation. By accepting Nephi's promise of freedom and a place in their community, Zoram undergoes a profound personal transformation—from a servant bound by duty to an equal and trusted member of the group, fully embracing his new identity within the covenant community. This shift emphasizes the importance of loyalty and trust in building and maintaining cohesive relationships, particularly within new or changing environments.

Adaptation to New Beliefs and Environments

Zoram's integration into Lehi's family also illustrates the challenges and rewards of embracing new beliefs and social groups. His willingness to leave behind his former life, including possibly his cultural and religious heritage, and to adopt new ways of living and believing highlights a flexible and open-minded approach to life's unpredictable changes. This aspect of Zoram's story invites us to consider our responses to new ideas and environments—are we open and adaptable, or resistant and closed off?

Role of Divine Guidance in Decision-Making

Zoram's acceptance of Nephi's explanation that God commanded their actions suggests a recognition of and respect for divine influence in his life decisions. This acknowledgment is crucial, as it points to the broader theme of seeking and recognizing divine guidance in our lives. Zoram's story encourages us to seek spiritual insights and to consider divine will in our decision-making processes, especially in moments of significant change or uncertainty.

In sum, Zoram's narrative, while secondary in the larger scriptural context, provides valuable insights into the dynamics of trust, loyalty, and personal evolution within the framework of divine guidance and community integration. His example serves as a testament to the transformative power of faith and fellowship and challenges us to remain open to the changes and divine directions we might encounter in our own lives.

Ishmael: A Figure of Unity and Endurance

Ishmael, a notable elder from Jerusalem **(1 Nephi 7:2-7; 16:7-19)**, plays a crucial role in the narrative of the Book of Mormon by joining Lehi's family in their exodus from Jerusalem and into the wilderness. His willingness to leave Jerusalem with his entire family after being approached by Nephi and his brothers illustrates his openness and responsiveness to divine callings, qualities deeply resonant with Christlike obedience and faith. Moreover, Ishmael's role in facilitating the intermarriage of his children with Lehi's children showcases his commitment to forging unity and strengthening familial bonds—traits that underscore a Christlike love and foresight for building a covenant community.

Ishmael also exhibits considerable patience and endurance, particularly evident during the arduous journey through the desert toward the promised land. His ability to endure not only the physical hardships of the journey but also the emotional and spiritual challenges, including the murmuring and rebellion from both his and Lehi's children, highlights his long-suffering and perseverance.

Lessons and Teachings from Ishmael's Life

Ishmael's interactions with Lehi's family and the experiences shared between the two families during their journey offer profound lessons on faith, unity, and the importance of communal bonds in overcoming adversity.

Faith and Obedience in Uncertain Times

Ishmael's decision to join Lehi on a perilous journey into the unknown demonstrates immense faith and trust in God's promises. This act of leaving behind everything familiar based on the testimony and urging of another family speaks volumes about the depth of his spiritual conviction. This scenario invites us to reflect on our readiness to act on faith, especially when it means stepping into the unknown based on divine assurances conveyed through others.

Building Unity through Trials

The journey of Ishmael's and Lehi's families through the wilderness is fraught with trials, including physical hardships and interpersonal conflicts. However, the eventual intermarriages between the members of the two families symbolize a unification that strengthens their communal bonds and ensures their collective survival and success. This teaches us the value of forging and maintaining strong relationships, particularly within faith communities, as a means to withstand and overcome collective challenges.

Endurance and Long-Suffering

Ishmael's endurance until his death during the journey (1 Nephi 16:34) showcases his commitment to the divine vision that guided their journey despite the numerous hardships faced. His example is a powerful testament to the virtue of long-suffering—a Christlike attribute that involves remaining steadfast in faith and purpose, even in the face of great personal loss and difficulty.

In sum, Ishmael's narrative offers valuable insights into the dynamics of faith-driven decisions, the building of community through shared trials, and the power of enduring commitment. His life serves as a reminder of the impact our choices have on our families and communities, encouraging a deeper engagement with the principles of unity, faith, and perseverance in our personal and collective spiritual journeys.

Ishmael's Wife: A Testament to Quiet Strength and Faith

Ishmael's wife, whose story is subtly woven into the fabric of the Book of Mormon **(1 Nephi 7:19)**, demonstrates Christlike attributes of faith, perseverance, and loyalty. Her journey from Jerusalem into the wilderness alongside her husband and family highlights her courage and steadfastness. In her willingness to leave behind a familiar life and face the uncertainties of a wilderness journey, she exemplifies a deep commitment to her family and to the divine directives they followed, embodying the virtues of support, sacrifice, and unconditional love.

Lessons and Teachings from the Life of Ishmael's Wife

Strength in Support and Sacrifice

Ishmael's wife's decision to support her husband's decision to join Lehi's family on their journey to the promised land speaks volumes about her inner strength and sacrificial spirit. Her support was crucial in maintaining the unity and morale of her family during their trials in the wilderness. Her story reminds us that within a family unit, support and sacrifice are invaluable. Often, it is the quiet strength and unwavering support of individuals like Ishmael's wife that ensure the well-being and progression of the entire group, highlighting the unsung but vital roles that sustain us through life's challenges.

Faith and Courage Amidst Uncertainty

Venturing into the unknown wilderness required not just physical endurance but immense faith and courage. Ishmael's wife's journey from Jerusalem into the wilderness is a profound testament to living a life of faith. Her ability to trust in divine promises, despite visible uncertainties, provides a powerful lesson on the essence of faith, which often involves stepping into the unknown with the belief that God will guide and provide.

Resilience in Adversity

Throughout the challenging journey in the wilderness, and as seen through the trials faced by Lehi's and Ishmael's families, Ishmael's wife likely had to harness great resilience. This resilience is a crucial attribute for anyone facing difficult circumstances. Her example prompts us to reflect on our own resilience in the face of life's adversities. How do we react to challenges and uncertainties? Do we respond with faith and courage, and how do we support others in their times of trial?

Legacy of Faith and Commitment

Ultimately, Ishmael's wife's journey contributed significantly to the legacy left by those who would establish a righteous civilization in a new land. Her commitment helped lay a foundation of faithfulness and perseverance. This legacy challenges us to consider what legacies we are creating through our daily actions and decisions. Are we contributing to a legacy of faith and righteousness that will benefit future generations?

In sum, while Ishmael's wife may not be a prominently featured character in the Book of Mormon, her life and actions provide profound lessons in faith, support, resilience, and the power of an individual's legacy. Her example serves as a beacon for all who face uncertainty and adversity, reminding us of the strength found in faith and the impact of our support and sacrifices on those around us.

Daughter of Ishmael: A Model of Loyalty and Faith

Ishmael's daughter, mentioned in the Book of Mormon **(1 Nephi 7:19; 16:7)**, exemplifies significant Christlike attributes such as loyalty, courage, and faith. During a critical moment in their wilderness journey, she, alongside her mother and other women, defended Nephi from the wrath of her brothers (1 Nephi 7:19). This act of defending Nephi not only shows her physical courage but also her spiritual insight and commitment to the prophetic leadership and divine mission of Lehi's family. Her potential later marriage to Nephi suggests a continued dedication to her faith and to the foundational families of the Nephite and Lamanite nations.

Lessons and Teachings from the Life of Ishmael's Daughter

Courage in the Face of Adversity

The act of defending Nephi against her own brothers' violent intentions is a profound display of courage. Ishmael's daughter's ability to stand up for what is right, even against family members, teaches us the importance of moral courage and conviction. Her example challenges us to consider how we might act courageously in our own lives, particularly when standing up for what is right means going against popular opinion or even facing familial pressures. In today's world, where conformity often overshadows conviction, her courage serves as a timeless reminder of the importance of staying true to our principles.

Faith and Loyalty

Her defense of Nephi, coupled with her weeping for the suffering of her group, illustrates a deep faith in the divine mission entrusted to Lehi's and Nephi's leadership. It also shows loyalty not only to her immediate family but to her spiritual leaders and the larger vision of their journey. Reflecting on this, we learn the value of faith and loyalty in our leaders and divine missions. Are we as steadfast in our faith and as loyal in our commitments, even when faced with personal trials and societal challenges?

Support and Empathy

The emotional support Ishmael's daughter provides—evidenced by her mourning over the tribulations faced by her group—highlights her empathetic nature. This empathy is crucial in leadership and community building, as it fosters understanding and unity among group members. This teaches us the importance of empathy in our interactions and leadership, reminding us to always consider the hardships of others and to offer support where possible.

Role in Building Foundations

Ishmael's daughter's actions and decisions, including her marriage to Nephi, played a foundational role in the establishment of the Nephite and Lamanite nations. Her life illustrates how individual actions can have long-term effects on community building and cultural development. Reflecting on this, we might consider how our personal decisions and actions contribute to the foundations of our communities. What kind of legacy are we building through our daily choices and behaviors?

In sum, while details about Ishmael's daughter are sparse in the Book of Mormon, her actions provide powerful lessons in courage, faith, loyalty, empathy, and the impact of personal decisions on broader community outcomes. Her example serves as an inspiration for all who seek to act righteously and courageously, contributing positively to their communities and adhering faithfully to their beliefs.

Author's Reflection

As I reflect on the lives of Zoram, Ishmael, Ishmael's Wife, and the Daughter of Ishmael, I am struck by the critical roles they played in the journey to the promised land. Their lives are not just background details in the larger narrative of Lehi's family; they are integral to the foundation of faith that sustained the group through trials and uncertainties. Each character embodies distinct virtues— loyalty, unity, strength, and faith—that are as essential today in our personal and communal lives as they were in ancient times.

Zoram: A Study in Loyalty and Integration

Zoram, initially a servant of Laban, becomes a pivotal figure in the story of Lehi's family. His decision to join Nephi and his brothers after recognizing their divine mission (1 Nephi 4:31-35) marks a significant turning point in his life. Zoram's loyalty, once established, proves to be unwavering. His swift integration into the family, despite his status as a foreigner and a former servant, underscores the power of genuine commitment and the ability to transcend past identities. Zoram's journey from outsider to insider challenges us to embrace and support those who seek to join our communities, recognizing that their contributions can significantly enrich our collective path.

Reflecting on Zoram's life, I see a powerful example of loyalty and the transformative power of faith. His willingness to leave behind his former life and join Nephi's family is a testament to his ability to recognize and embrace truth, even when it means significant personal risk. In modern life, Zoram's example challenges us to consider how we respond when faced with opportunities to align ourselves with truth and righteousness. Are we willing to leave behind our comfort zones, as Zoram did, to join in a greater cause? Zoram's integration into the family also reminds us of the importance of embracing and supporting newcomers in our communities, recognizing that their loyalty and contributions can strengthen the collective journey toward our own promised lands.

Ishmael: A Figure of Unity and Endurance

Ishmael's decision to join Lehi's family on their journey to the promised land (1 Nephi 7:4-5) highlights his role as a unifying figure. His family's inclusion was crucial for the survival and continuity of Lehi's group, providing the necessary partnerships for building a new community. Ishmael's willingness to leave Jerusalem, despite his age and the challenges of the journey, not only demonstrates his endurance and commitment to the divine mission but also sets a powerful example for future generations, showing that true faith often requires sacrifice and steadfastness across all stages of life.

Ishmael's life offers profound lessons in unity and endurance. His decision to support Lehi, even at the cost of leaving everything behind, exemplifies the strength of his faith and his deep understanding of the importance of unity in fulfilling divine purposes. In today's context, Ishmael's example encourages us to prioritize the collective good over personal comfort, reminding us that true unity often requires significant personal sacrifice.

In our personal and communal lives, Ishmael's example challenges us to prioritize unity and collective well-being, even when it requires personal sacrifice. His endurance through the difficulties of the journey reminds us that achieving our promised lands—whether they be spiritual goals, family unity, or communal peace—requires perseverance and a commitment to the collective good.

Ishmael's Wife: A Testament to Quiet Strength and Faith

Ishmael's wife, though not mentioned by name, plays a crucial role in supporting her family during their journey. Her presence is a stabilizing force, providing the quiet strength necessary to keep the family together during times of trial and uncertainty. The fact that she and her daughters joined the journey to the promised land speaks to her deep faith and trust in her husband's decision and the divine mission of Lehi's family.

Reflecting on Ishmael's wife, I see a powerful example of quiet strength and unwavering faith. Her willingness to follow her husband into the unknown, supporting him and their children through the hardships of the journey, underscores the often understated yet vital role of women in sustaining family and community through faith. Ishmael's wife's quiet resilience serves as a lasting influence on the community's endurance and success, reminding us of the enduring impact of unwavering support and faith.

In today's world, her example reminds us of the often-overlooked but essential role that quiet strength and support play in achieving collective goals. Ishmael's wife challenges us to recognize and honor the contributions of those who, like her, provide the foundation of faith and stability that enables communities to thrive and reach their promised lands.

Daughter of Ishmael: A Model of Loyalty and Faith

The Daughter of Ishmael, like her mother, embodies loyalty and faith. Her marriage to one of Lehi's sons (1 Nephi 16:7) symbolizes the unification of the families and the strengthening of the group's collective identity. Her journey with her family to the promised land, despite the challenges and uncertainties, reflects her deep faith in the divine mission of Lehi's family and her commitment to the collective journey.

Reflecting on the Daughter of Ishmael, I am reminded of the importance of loyalty and faith in sustaining family and community. Her decision to marry into Lehi's family and to fully commit to their journey exemplifies the kind of loyalty that is essential for the success of any collective endeavor. In our modern lives, her example challenges us to actively consider our contributions to the unity and strength of our families and communities. Like the Daughter of Ishmael, we are called to fully commit to our roles, understanding that our loyalty and faith are foundational in building strong, resilient communities capable of withstanding the trials of time.

Are we, like the Daughter of Ishmael, willing to fully commit to our roles and support the collective journey toward our shared goals? Her faith in the face of uncertainty also reminds us that true loyalty is rooted in faith—faith in God, in our loved ones, and in the collective mission we share.

Summary

The characters of Chapter 3—Zoram, Ishmael, Ishmael's Wife, and the Daughter of Ishmael—each offer unique insights into the virtues of loyalty, unity, strength, and faith. Their lives provide powerful examples of how these virtues are essential in the journey toward promised lands, whether those lands are physical, spiritual, or communal.

Zoram's loyalty and integration remind us of the transformative power of embracing truth and the importance of supporting newcomers in our communities. Ishmael's role as a unifying figure and his endurance through trials challenge us to prioritize unity and collective well-being. Ishmael's wife's quiet strength and unwavering faith highlight the vital role of women in sustaining family and community through difficult times. The Daughter of Ishmael's loyalty and faith exemplify the importance of commitment to the collective mission and the power of faith in overcoming uncertainty.

As I reflect on the lives of Zoram, Ishmael, Ishmael's Wife, and the Daughter of Ishmael, I am inspired not only to cultivate these virtues in my own life but also to actively contribute to the unity, strength, and faith of my community. Their stories remind us that the journey to our promised lands—whether personal, spiritual, or communal—requires not only individual effort but a collective commitment to shared values and goals.

By drawing upon the experiences of Zoram, Ishmael, Ishmael's Wife, and the Daughter of Ishmael, we equip ourselves to face the trials and opportunities that lie ahead with greater resilience and unity. Their lives remind us that our journey toward our own promised lands is strengthened when we are steadfast in faith, committed to collective well-being, and guided by the virtues that sustain us through every challenge.

Part II

Leadership and Legacy –

Navigating a New World

Part II delves into the pivotal leadership roles that guided the Nephite civilization through its crucial formative years in the promised land. These leaders, both secular and spiritual, were tasked with the monumental challenge of establishing a new society in an unfamiliar world. This section includes two chapters that thoroughly examine the dual pillars of leadership—secular governance and spiritual stewardship—that were essential in establishing a cohesive society, maintaining religious continuity, and ensuring the survival and prosperity of the Nephite people in their new environment.

These chapters are fundamental to Part II as they highlight the crucial decisions and enduring legacies of the leaders who successfully navigated the complexities of a new world, leaving a profound impact on both their contemporaries and future generations. Their foresight and wisdom were pivotal in ensuring not only the immediate survival of the Nephite people but also their long-term prosperity and cultural continuity. Together, these two chapters offer a comprehensive exploration of the leadership and legacy that forged the Nephite civilization. By examining both the decisions of rulers and the efforts of record keepers, we gain insight into how these figures crafted a resilient society capable of withstanding the trials of a new world.

These chapters illustrate the indispensable roles of rulers and record keepers in steering the Nephite people through uncharted territory. Their efforts in establishing governance and preserving the spiritual and historical heritage not only defined Nephite society but also laid the foundation for its enduring legacy. As we explore the contributions of these influential leaders, we uncover the timeless principles that not only sustained a civilization in its infancy but also continue to resonate and inspire effective leadership in our world today.

Chapter 4

Secular and Spiritual Leaders

Upon arriving in the promised land, the Nephites confronted the daunting challenge of building a stable and enduring society. This task required a careful balance between secular governance and spiritual leadership as the community sought to navigate the complexities of their new environment. This chapter delves into the lives and contributions of the Second King of the Nephites, Mosiah, the Leader of Zarahemla, and King Benjamin. These leaders played crucial roles in navigating the challenges of a new society, ensuring both the temporal welfare and spiritual growth of their people.

Historical Context

After their arduous journey from Jerusalem to the promised land, Lehi's family and their descendants faced the monumental task of building a new civilization. During this pivotal period in Nephite history, the fledgling society stood at a crossroads. Strong, visionary leadership was essential to navigating the trials of establishing order, enacting just laws, and providing spiritual guidance in a land rife with both opportunities and uncertainties. The figures in this chapter exemplify the blend of secular and spiritual responsibilities that were essential for the survival and prosperity of the Nephite people.

Characters in Chapter 4

- **Second King of the Nephites** ~ Tasked with the daunting responsibility of succeeding Nephi, this unnamed king worked to uphold and extend Nephi's legacy, striving to balance secular governance with the spiritual tenets that had guided his predecessor.
- **Mosiah** ~ A leader of exceptional foresight, Mosiah led the Nephites from their ancestral land to Zarahemla, uniting diverse peoples under a single, righteous community.
- **Leader of Zarahemla** ~ An emblem of humility and strength, this leader welcomed Mosiah's people, facilitating

a peaceful integration that would ensure the future stability of both groups.

- **King Benjamin** ~ A paragon of servant leadership, King Benjamin's reign was marked by his teachings on humility, service, and living a Christ-centered life.

This historical context provides a backdrop for understanding the critical roles these leaders played in shaping Nephite society. Through their actions and teachings, these leaders not only shaped the immediate future of the Nephite civilization but also left behind timeless lessons on the integration of spiritual and temporal responsibilities, the power of unity and humility in governance, and the enduring importance of righteous leadership. These leaders not only ensured the survival and prosperity of their people but also laid the groundwork for a society that valued both divine commandments and practical wisdom.

Second King of the Nephites: A Legacy of Righteous Leadership

Following in Nephi's footsteps, the Second King of the Nephites **(Jacob 1:9-11)** inherited the formidable responsibility of preserving and extending the legacy of a righteous leader. His reign underscores the critical importance of continuity in leadership, particularly during times of transition. He embodied Christlike attributes essential for wise and just leadership. This king, who remains unnamed in the scriptures, likely exhibited traits of humility, fairness, and devotion, as he was selected by Nephi, a prophet known for his righteousness and prophetic leadership. The king's commitment to continuing Nephi's legacy suggests a strong adherence to the principles of gospel living and a dedication to serving his people with equity and spiritual integrity.

Lessons and Teachings from the Reign of the Second King of the Nephites

Spiritual and Secular Leadership: Transition and Continuity

The smooth transition of leadership from Nephi to the second king highlights the importance of thoughtful succession planning. Nephi's choice was likely guided by both the individual's personal virtues and his capability to lead according to the established divine mandates. This teaches us the critical nature of leadership transitions in any organization or community and the need for careful selection based on both character and competence. Reflecting on this, leaders today can appreciate the importance of preparing for leadership succession to ensure continuity and stability.

Upholding Foundational Values

The second king's commitment to upholding the laws and teachings established by Nephi underscores the importance of foundational values in leadership. Just as Nephi had set a precedent for righteousness and obedience to God's commandments, his successor's role was to continue these principles, ensuring that the spiritual and societal laws were neither diluted nor disregarded. This aspect of his leadership reminds us of the responsibility leaders have to maintain and reinforce core values, fostering a culture of integrity and righteousness.

Servant Leadership

As a king appointed in a theocratic society, the second king would have been expected to exemplify servant leadership—prioritizing the welfare of his people over personal gain. This aligns with Christlike leadership, which emphasizes service, compassion, and humility. Reflecting on this, we can evaluate our approaches to leadership and influence. Do we lead by serving others? Are our decisions and actions benefiting those we lead?

Resilience in Governance

Given the challenges of external threats and internal dissent, the second king's ability to maintain unity and order would have required significant resilience and strategic governance. His reign would teach us about the necessity of resilience in leadership, particularly in maintaining peace and unity in the face of adversity. This invites current and aspiring leaders to consider how they manage conflict and opposition, emphasizing the need for strategies that promote long-term peace and cohesion.

In sum, while the specific details of the second king's reign are sparse, the implications of his leadership following Nephi offer rich lessons in leadership transition, the upholding of foundational values, servant leadership, and resilience in governance. These lessons are invaluable for anyone in a position of influence, prompting a reflection on how we can embody these principles to effect positive change and maintain continuity in our respective spheres. As the Nephite society continued to evolve, the integration of secular and spiritual leadership became even more pronounced, as seen in the life and reign of Mosiah.

Mosiah: A Leader of Faith and Vision

Mosiah, a key figure in the Book of Mormon **(Omni 1:12-23)**, demonstrates several Christlike attributes that define him as a leader of great faith and vision. His decision to lead his people out of the land of Nephi to find a new home in Zarahemla is indicative of his courage, wisdom, and trust in divine guidance. Mosiah's leadership is characterized by his proactive approach to seeking safety and prosperity for his people, his ability to unite and integrate different groups, and his dedication to maintaining and sharing the religious records, which solidify their cultural and spiritual identity.

Lessons and Teachings from Mosiah's Life and Actions

Leadership in Transition

Mosiah's journey from the land of Nephi to Zarahemla illustrates the challenges and opportunities inherent in leading during times of transition. His ability to guide his people through physical and cultural shifts demonstrates the importance of leadership that is adaptable, visionary, and grounded in faith. This story is particularly instructive for leaders in all spheres today, highlighting the need to anticipate changes, prepare people for them, and manage them with foresight and integrity.

Unity Through Integration

Upon arriving in Zarahemla, Mosiah not only merges his followers with the existing inhabitants but also takes significant steps to integrate their cultures and histories. He instructs the people of Zarahemla on the Nephite language and unifies them under a new religious and governmental structure. This integration effort teaches us the value of inclusivity and the importance of embracing diversity within a unified framework, aiming for a cohesive society that respects and incorporates various cultural backgrounds.

The Role of Records in Preserving Identity

Mosiah's commitment to maintaining and teaching from the Nephite records underscores the crucial role that written histories and religious texts play in preserving a people's identity and spiritual foundation. This aspect of his leadership emphasizes the importance of records and education in maintaining cultural continuity and moral integrity. It invites us to reflect on how we preserve and utilize our own historical and spiritual legacies to educate and guide future generations.

Faith and Obedience to Divine Will

Throughout his journey, Mosiah exhibits a profound faith in God's guidance, which is evident in his decision to lead his people to a new land. His actions remind us of the importance of seeking divine will in our decisions and the power of faith to guide us through uncertainty. This lesson challenges us to consider the role of faith in our personal and communal decisions, inspiring us to seek and follow divine guidance in our endeavors.

In sum, Mosiah's story provides powerful insights into effective leadership, the importance of unity and cultural integration, the vital role of records in maintaining a community's identity, and the transformative power of faith and obedience. His example offers valuable lessons for leaders and communities today, emphasizing the need for vision, adaptability, and spiritual grounding in navigating the challenges of change and diversity.

Leader of Zarahemla: A Profile of Strength and Leadership

The leader of Zarahemla, described briefly in the Book of Omni as a "strong and mighty man," likely embodies the Christlike virtues of courage, strength, and wisdom. His portrayal suggests a leader who was not only physically robust but also strong in his convictions and leadership qualities. This combination of physical and moral strength is emblematic of Christlike leadership, which involves protecting and guiding one's people with both compassion and authority.

Lessons and Teachings from the Leadership of the Leader of Zarahemla

The Role of Physical and Moral Strength in Leadership

The description of the leader of Zarahemla as a "strong and mighty man" highlights the importance of physical presence and moral strength in leadership. Effective leaders often embody a blend of these qualities, using their physical presence to command respect and their moral strength to inspire trust and confidence. This duality teaches us the value of developing both aspects in our own leadership styles—ensuring that we are strong enough to protect and assertive enough to guide, yet also wise and moral to lead with integrity.

Adaptability and Openness to Integration

The leader of Zarahemla's willingness to integrate his people with Mosiah's followers underlines the importance of adaptability and openness in leadership. Facing a group with preserved language and records, the leader of Zarahemla shows commendable flexibility by merging his people with Mosiah's, recognizing the benefits of unified religious and cultural practices. This adaptability is a vital lesson for leaders in any context, emphasizing the need to be open to new ideas and changes that can enrich and enhance the community's well-being.

Preservation and Revival of Cultural Identity

The integration of the people of Zarahemla with Mosiah's group also involves a significant cultural and religious revival. The leader's role in this process teaches us the importance of preserving cultural identity and embracing opportunities for renewal. Leaders must be custodians of their community's heritage while also being agents of positive change, balancing tradition with innovation. This role challenges us to consider how we handle the preservation of our own cultural and spiritual identities while remaining receptive to renewal and growth.

Unity Through Shared Heritage and Values

Finally, the leader of Zarahemla's experience underscores the power of shared heritage and values in forging unity. His acceptance of Mosiah's leadership, based on their shared descent and spiritual beliefs, demonstrates how common ground can be used to unite disparate groups. This teaches us to seek and cultivate shared values and common histories in our endeavors to build cohesive communities or teams.

In conclusion, the leader of Zarahemla, though only briefly mentioned, offers profound insights into the nature of leadership that combines strength, adaptability, and a commitment to cultural and spiritual unity. His actions during a critical period of integration provide valuable lessons on the qualities necessary for effective and transformative leadership.

King Benjamin: A Legacy of Righteous Leadership

King Benjamin, succeeding his father Mosiah as king of Zarahemla, exemplifies Christlike attributes that epitomize wise and benevolent leadership. He is known for his humility, dedication to his people's welfare, and deep spirituality. As he receives the Nephite records from his father, his commitment to preserving their history and teachings reflects his profound respect for his heritage and his understanding of the importance of these records in maintaining the spiritual foundation of his people.

Lessons and Teachings from King Benjamin's Early Reign

The Importance of Spiritual and Secular Knowledge

The transfer of Nephite records to King Benjamin highlights the dual role of the king as both a secular leader and a spiritual guide. This illustrates the inseparable connection between governance and spirituality in Nephite society, where the king is expected to lead in both civic and religious capacities. From this, we learn the importance of leaders possessing both secular and spiritual knowledge. Reflecting on this, we can appreciate the value of a well-rounded education and understanding in our leaders today, encouraging those in positions of influence to cultivate both types of knowledge to serve effectively.

Stewardship of Cultural Heritage

King Benjamin's reception of the records underscores his role as a steward of his people's cultural and religious heritage. This stewardship is essential not only for maintaining historical continuity but also for upholding and imparting the spiritual values contained in the records. The lesson here is that all individuals, especially leaders, have a responsibility to preserve and promote their cultural and spiritual legacies. This prompts us to consider how we are preserving our own heritage—what actions are we undertaking to ensure that valuable traditions and teachings are not lost to future generations?

Unity Through Shared History

By maintaining and emphasizing the importance of the Nephite records, King Benjamin also plays a crucial role in fostering unity among his people. The records serve as a common thread that links diverse groups within his kingdom, highlighting shared histories and values. This teaches us the power of shared stories and histories in uniting disparate groups. Reflecting on this, it is worth considering how shared narratives and histories can be used in our communities to promote understanding and cohesion.

Preparation for Responsible Leadership

The way Benjamin receives and handles the records shows his preparation and readiness for leadership. This transition period is critical, as it sets the stage for his subsequent actions as king, which are marked by wisdom and righteousness. The lesson here is the importance of preparation and readiness in leadership. Effective leadership transitions are crucial for maintaining continuity and stability, prompting us to ensure that new leaders are well-prepared to take on their roles.

In sum, King Benjamin's early actions, as recorded in Omni, provide profound insights into the integration of spiritual and secular duties, the importance of stewarding cultural heritage, the unifying power of shared history, and the crucial nature of leadership preparation. These lessons from Benjamin's reception of the Nephite records are timeless and applicable across various leadership contexts today, encouraging a balanced, informed, and conscientious approach to leadership roles.

Author's Reflection

Reflecting on the lives of the Second King of the Nephites, Mosiah, the Leader of Zarahemla, and King Benjamin, I am struck by the powerful examples of leadership and righteousness they each demonstrate. These leaders are not just historical figures; they are embodiments of the principles of faith, service, and governance that are essential for building and sustaining any community, especially one seeking to achieve its own "promised land." Each character provides unique insights into the responsibilities and challenges of leadership, as well as the importance of aligning one's governance with divine principles.

Second King of the Nephites: The Legacy of Righteous Leadership

The Second King of the Nephites, who followed Nephi in leadership, is a figure whose life underscores the importance of continuity in righteous governance. Although less detailed in scripture, his actions as described in Jacob 1:9-10 highlight a commitment to the values and teachings established by Nephi. He is noted for maintaining the spiritual and political stability of the Nephite people, ensuring that the foundations laid by Nephi were preserved.

Reflecting on the Second King's life, I see a model of leadership that prioritizes the preservation of righteous traditions and the continuity of faith. In modern contexts, this example challenges leaders to consider how they can sustain and build upon the legacies of their predecessors while remaining true to core principles. The Second King's leadership reminds us that achieving and sustaining our promised lands requires not just innovative leadership but also a deep respect for the spiritual and ethical foundations that support our communities. His life encourages us to value continuity in leadership and the importance of nurturing what has been divinely established.

Mosiah: A Leader of Faith and Vision

Mosiah, as described in the Book of Mormon, is a leader who exemplifies both spiritual insight and practical governance. He leads the Nephites from the land of Nephi to Zarahemla (Omni 1:12-14), a journey that symbolizes not just a physical relocation but a spiritual transition to a place of greater safety and prosperity. Mosiah's leadership is marked by his ability to unify diverse groups, as seen in the successful integration of the Nephites with the people of Zarahemla.

Mosiah's life offers profound lessons in leadership, particularly in the importance of vision and faith in guiding a community toward its promised land. His decision to lead the people out of the land of Nephi, despite the inherent risks, reflects a deep trust in divine guidance and an understanding of the greater good. In today's world, Mosiah's example challenges leaders to be visionary, to see beyond immediate challenges, and to guide their people with faith and foresight. His successful unification of different groups also teaches us the importance of inclusivity and the power of shared purpose in achieving communal goals.

Leader of Zarahemla: A Profile of Strength and Leadership

The Leader of Zarahemla, though not as prominently detailed as other leaders, plays a crucial role in the preservation and growth of his people. His willingness to unite with the Nephites under Mosiah's leadership (Omni 1:19) demonstrates both humility and wisdom. Recognizing the strengths that Mosiah brought to the table, the Leader of Zarahemla chose collaboration over competition, a decision that ensured the survival and prosperity of both peoples.

Reflecting on the Leader of Zarahemla, I am reminded of the importance of humility and the willingness to collaborate for the greater good. In modern contexts, leaders are often tempted to prioritize personal or political power over the collective well-being. The Leader of Zarahemla's example challenges us to recognize the value of collaboration and to put aside personal ambitions in favor *of what will best serve our communities. His life teaches us that true leadership sometimes involves stepping back and allowing others to lead when their vision and capabilities are aligned with the greater good.*

King Benjamin: A Legacy of Righteous Leadership

King Benjamin is one of the most revered figures in the Book of Mormon, known for his profound teachings and humble leadership. His speech to his people, as recorded in Mosiah 2-5, is a powerful discourse on service, humility, and the nature of true leadership. King Benjamin emphasizes that true greatness lies in serving others (Mosiah 2:17) and that leaders should not seek to elevate themselves above those they lead (Mosiah 2:26). His teachings about the Atonement and the necessity of spiritual rebirth (Mosiah 3:19) provide a spiritual foundation that resonates deeply with the principles of faith and repentance.

Reflecting on King Benjamin's life, I see a model of leadership that is deeply rooted in humility, service, and spiritual insight. His teachings challenge modern leaders to view their roles as opportunities to serve rather than to dominate. King Benjamin's life reminds us that the foundation of any promised land is built on the principles of service and humility, where leaders and followers alike are committed to the well-being of each other. His discourse on the Atonement also emphasizes the need for personal and communal repentance, reminding us that spiritual renewal is essential for the ongoing prosperity of any community.

Summary

The characters of Chapter 4—Second King of the Nephites, Mosiah, Leader of Zarahemla, and King Benjamin—each offer profound insights into the principles of righteous leadership and governance. Their lives provide timeless lessons that are essential for any community striving to achieve its promised land.

The Second King of the Nephites teaches us the value of continuity in leadership and the importance of preserving righteous foundations. Mosiah exemplifies visionary leadership and the power of faith and unity in guiding a community through transitions. The Leader of Zarahemla demonstrates the strength of humility and the wisdom of collaboration for the greater good. King Benjamin provides a powerful example of servant leadership, where humility, service, and spiritual insight form the bedrock of a prosperous and righteous society.

These leaders' lives challenge us to embody these principles in our own spheres of influence, whether in personal leadership, community engagement, or broader governance. As we reflect on their legacies, we are reminded that the pursuit of any promised land whether it be personal, communal, or societal, demands more than just vision and faith. It requires an unwavering commitment to the principles of service, unity, and righteous leadership. In our own spheres of influence, these examples challenge us to lead with integrity, to foster unity through collaboration, and to serve with humility and purpose.

Chapter 5

Guardians of Nephite Legacy: The Record Keepers

Entrusted with the sacred duty of preserving the spiritual and historical legacy of the Nephite people, a lineage of devoted record keepers played a pivotal role in safeguarding the teachings and prophecies that would guide future generations. This chapter explores the lives and contributions of Enos, Jarom, Omni, Amaron, Chemish, Abinadom, and Amaleki. Each of these individuals played a crucial role in maintaining the spiritual and historical continuity of the Nephite people through their meticulous record-keeping efforts.

Historical Context

The period covered by the record keepers in the Book of Omni spans several generations, from approximately 420 BC to 130 BC, a time that demanded continuous dedication to the sacred duty of preserving the Nephite heritage through turbulent and transformative years. This era was marked by significant social, political, and spiritual changes within Nephite society. The responsibility of preserving the sacred records, originally instituted by Nephi, was handed down through his descendants, ensuring that the teachings, prophecies, and history of the Nephites were meticulously documented for future generations.

Characters in Chapter 5

- **Enos** ~ Renowned for his fervent prayer, Enos exemplifies deep spiritual commitment and a dedication to the spiritual well-being of his people and their enemies.
- **Jarom** ~ A diligent steward, Jarom chronicled both the spiritual fortitude and military challenges faced by the Nephites, ensuring the preservation of their covenant relationship with God.
- **Omni** ~ Marked by humility, Omni candidly acknowledged his own spiritual struggles while faithfully maintaining the sacred records entrusted to him.

- **Amaron** ~ A witness to his people's moral decline, Amaron recorded the consequences of their wickedness, providing a stark reminder of divine justice.
- **Chemish** ~ A custodian of continuity, Chemish emphasized the importance of record authenticity and the seamless transmission of sacred knowledge across generations.
- **Abinadom** ~ A warrior and record keeper, Abinadom documented the military efforts to defend the Nephite nation, underscoring the physical and spiritual battles his people endured.
- **Amaleki** - A historian and unifier, Amaleki detailed the significant events that shaped the Nephite nation, including the merging with the people of Zarahemla, and ensured the records' preservation for future generations.

Through the ages, these record keepers ensured that the spiritual and historical threads of Nephite society were woven together, each contributing to a tapestry of faith that would endure the test of time. Their combined efforts ensured that the teachings, prophecies, and experiences of their civilization were preserved, providing valuable lessons on faith, repentance, and the importance of divine guidance. The records they kept serve as a testament to their dedication and the enduring power of written testimony in preserving a people's spiritual heritage.

Enos: A Model of Devotion and Prayerful Commitment

Enos, the son of Jacob and grandson of Lehi **(Enos 1:1-27)** carries forward his family's spiritual legacy, exemplifying profound Christlike attributes primarily through his heartfelt and transformative prayer. Enos's story is particularly striking for its emphasis on personal conversion and the power of sincere communication with God. His transformative prayer not only shaped his personal faith but also set a precedent of spiritual dedication that would resonate through his descendants, reinforcing the Nephite commitment to divine communication. His attributes include a deep humility, earnest repentance, unwavering faith, and a fervent commitment to the welfare of both his people and his adversaries. These characteristics are vividly displayed in his lengthy solitary prayer, where he wrestles before God for a remission of his sins and subsequently prays with great zeal for his brethren and even for his enemies.

Lessons and Teachings from Enos's Life and Writings

The Power of Prayer

Enos's narrative is central to understanding the transformative power of sincere prayer. His initial, fervent plea for his own soul and his subsequent intercessions for his people and even his enemies illustrate the profound impact that prayer can have not only on the supplicant but also on the broader community. Enos's experience teaches us that prayer is not a passive activity but a vigorous spiritual endeavor that can lead to significant personal and communal transformations. This story invites us to reflect on the depth and sincerity of our prayers. Are we merely reciting words, or are we engaging in a meaningful dialogue with God that has the power to transform?

Legacy of Faith and Concern for Others

Enos not only prays for himself but also shows a remarkable concern for the spiritual and physical well-being of his friends and foes alike. His prayers extend to the Lamanites, who were at odds with his people, reflecting a Christlike love for one's enemies. This extension of concern beyond immediate kin and community underscores the universal scope of Christian charity and presents a challenge to expand our circles of concern, praying earnestly for and actively seeking the good of those beyond our immediate affiliations.

Stewardship of Spiritual Knowledge

Enos's diligence in preserving the records and ensuring their continuance among his people highlights his understanding of stewardship over spiritual knowledge. His commitment to record-keeping and transmission of the gospel legacy reflects an awareness of the importance of sacred histories and teachings for maintaining faith across generations. This aspect of Enos's life prompts us to consider our role in preserving and transmitting spiritual and moral wisdom. How are we contributing to the spiritual legacy that will guide future generations?

Enduring Faith in Divine Promises

Throughout his writings, Enos expresses a steadfast trust in God's promises, particularly regarding the preservation of the records and the eventual restoration of the gospel among the Lamanites. His unwavering faith in the face of long odds serves as a testament to the power of holding firm in divine assurances, even when their fulfillment lies far in the future. Reflecting on this, we are encouraged to hold fast to God's promises in our lives, trusting in His timing and faithfulness.

In sum, Enos's life and teachings offer profound insights into the nature of prayer, the breadth of Christian charity, the responsibilities of stewardship, and the resilience of faith. His narrative encourages a deeper engagement with our spiritual practices, urging us to cultivate a prayer life that transforms, to embrace a more inclusive love, to responsibly handle spiritual knowledge, and to trust unwaveringly in divine promises.

Jarom: A Steward of Record and Righteousness

Jarom, the son of Enos **(Jarom 1:1-15)**, is a minor but significant figure in the Book of Mormon who exemplifies diligence, faithfulness, and commitment to divine commandments. As the keeper of the small plates after his father, Jarom's stewardship and integrity in maintaining the records are pivotal for preserving the Nephite history and teachings. Though his words are few, Jarom's dedication to his role as both a guardian of the records and a protector of his people's spiritual well-being is evident, reflecting a deep sense of duty that transcended his personal contributions. Jarom's actions reflect Christlike attributes of stewardship, perseverance, and an active commitment to upholding righteousness among his community.

Lessons and Teachings from Jarom's Life and Writings

The Vital Role of Spiritual and Temporal Stewardship

Jarom's dual role as a spiritual leader and a civic participant illustrates the interconnectedness of spiritual and temporal duties. His commitment to maintaining the records aligns with his efforts to uphold the Nephite laws and defend his people. This dual stewardship emphasizes the principle that spiritual well-being cannot be divorced from temporal security and prosperity.

Reflecting on this, we can learn the importance of balancing our spiritual commitments with civic responsibilities, recognizing that each influence and supports the other.

Perseverance in Upholding Traditions and Records

Despite recognizing that his contributions to the plates were small, Jarom's perseverance in keeping the records highlights a profound respect for tradition and obedience to divine commandments. His acknowledgment that his role, though seemingly minor, was part of a larger divine purpose teaches us the value of faithfulness in small duties. This lesson invites us to consider how we treat responsibilities that might seem insignificant but are integral to larger purposes. Are we diligent and faithful, even in seemingly small tasks?

Active Defense of Beliefs and Community

Jarom's involvement in defending his people against Lamanite attacks underscores the necessity at times to actively defend one's beliefs and community. This active defense is both physical, in terms of military engagement, and spiritual, through the promotion of righteousness and religious integrity among his people. The lesson here extends to the modern imperative to stand up for one's beliefs and communities in both tangible and intangible ways, advocating for and defending the principles that sustain communal life and spiritual health.

Continuity and Change in Religious Leadership

Finally, Jarom's transition of the records to his own son, Omni, symbolizes the ongoing chain of religious leadership and the importance of preparing future generations to take on roles of spiritual leadership. This aspect of his life reminds us of the importance of mentorship and succession in any vital endeavor, encouraging us to prepare those who follow us to continue the work we have begun.

In sum, Jarom's contributions, while briefly documented, offer rich insights into the practice of diligent stewardship, the balance of spiritual and civic duties, and the importance of defending and transmitting core values. His life encourages a reevaluation of our commitments and responsibilities, inspiring us to engage more fully in our communities with a balanced approach that honors both our spiritual values and our temporal realities.

Omni: A Link in the Chain of Nephite Record Keepers

Omni, a descendant of Jarom and a brief custodian of the Nephite records **(Omni 1:1-3)**, presents a complex figure in the Book of Mormon. While his personal contributions to the records are scant, the few verses he writes are revealing. Omni confesses his own shortcomings, stating that he is "a wicked man" and that he has not kept the statutes and commandments of the Lord as he should have (Omni 1:2). This admission shows a degree of self-awareness and humility, characteristics that are crucial for spiritual growth and repentance. Despite these personal struggles, Omni fulfills his duty in maintaining and passing on the sacred records, demonstrating a commitment to his lineage's responsibility and an acknowledgment of the importance of this divine charge.

Lessons and Teachings from Omni's Brief Account

The Challenge of Spiritual Leadership in Times of Turmoil

Omni's account, though brief, highlights the significant challenges of maintaining spiritual duties amidst societal turmoil and personal failings. His struggle to adhere to God's commandments, juxtaposed with his role as a record keeper, underscores the difficulties that arise when external pressures collide with personal and spiritual responsibilities. These narrative invites reflection on how individuals today manage the tension between personal spiritual growth and external responsibilities, especially in challenging times. It encourages a contemplation of resilience and the importance of seeking divine help in fulfilling our duties.

Integrity in Admitting Shortcomings

Omni's admission of his spiritual shortcomings is a profound lesson in humility and integrity. By acknowledging his weaknesses, he provides an honest account of his life and spiritual state, which is crucial for true repentance and improvement. This openness serves as a reminder of the importance of self-assessment in spiritual life, urging us to be honest about our faults while striving to fulfill our responsibilities. It challenges us to consider how we handle our own failings—do we acknowledge and work on them, or do we ignore and hide them?

The Importance of Maintaining Legacy Amidst Personal Imperfections

Despite acknowledging his faults, Omni ensures the continuation of the Nephite records by passing them to his son, Amaron. This act highlights the importance of maintaining spiritual and cultural legacies, even if one feels personally inadequate. Omni's decision to continue the tradition of record-keeping, despite his self-confessed wickedness, teaches that our efforts to preserve valuable legacies can and should transcend our personal failings. This aspect of his narrative prompts us to reflect on how we contribute to the continuation of valuable traditions and knowledge, regardless of our personal struggles.

The Role of Records in Preserving History and Faith

Omni's continuation of the record-keeping tradition underscores the vital role that records play in preserving history and faith across generations. His contribution, though minor, ensures that the chain of transmission remains unbroken, allowing future generations access to their heritage and the teachings of their ancestors. This teaches the importance of documentation and preservation of spiritual and historical knowledge, encouraging us to consider what records, stories, or teachings we are passing on to future generations.

In sum, Omni's brief entries in the Book of Mormon offer valuable lessons on the complexities of spiritual and temporal leadership, the importance of humility and honesty in personal growth, and the crucial role of maintaining cultural and spiritual legacies amidst personal and societal challenges. His story is a poignant reminder of the enduring impact of our actions, both in preserving traditions and in fostering honesty and integrity in our spiritual journeys.

Amaron, Chemish, Abinadom, and Amaleki: Brief Stewards of a Sacred Legacy

Amaron **(Omni 1:4)**, Chemish **(Omni 1:8-9)**, Abinadom **(Omni 1:10-11)**, and Amaleki **(Omni 1:12-25)** each exhibited Christlike attributes that underscored their roles as brief record keepers in the Book of Mormon. Their stewardship, though short-lived, demonstrated responsibility, faithfulness, and a profound respect for their sacred duty. Though their contributions were brief, these keepers ensured the unbroken chain of record-keeping, each adding a vital link to the preservation of Nephite history, faith, and culture. Each man, in his time, ensured the continuation of the record, a task that required diligence and a commitment to preserving their people's history and prophecies for future generations.

Informed Essay on Their Teachings and Lessons

Amaron - Preserving History Amidst Decline

Amaron's writings are succinct but significant. He notes the wickedness of the people in his day and the consequential divine judgment that led to their suffering (Omni 1:5). From Amaron, we learn the importance of historical awareness and the need to recognize divine justice in societal events. His entry teaches us that keeping a record of spiritual and societal conditions can serve as a warning and guide for future generations.

Chemish - Confirming the Handover

Chemish's entry is brief, primarily confirming his writing in the record after his brother Amaron and emphasizing the importance of the truthfulness of the record (Omni 1:9). Chemish teaches us about the importance of validation and continuity in record-keeping. His commitment to ensuring that the record was accurate and his acknowledgment of the record's familial transmission underscore the value of trustworthiness and responsibility in stewarding sacred duties.

Abinadom - Witness of Wars

Abinadom's account includes his personal involvement in the Nephite wars against the Lamanites (Omni 1:10). Unlike his predecessors, his contribution leans more on the physical defense of his people rather than their spiritual insights. From Abinadom, we learn the harsh realities of defending one's community and the burden of leadership during wartime. His record reminds us that our duties may require direct action and personal sacrifice, and these, too, are important to document and remember.

Amaleki - The Bridge to Stability

Amaleki's writings are more extensive, covering the discovery of the people of Zarahemla and the eventual migration of a group to the land of Nephi (Omni 1:12-25). He ends his record by transferring the plates to King Benjamin, ensuring their preservation. Amaleki teaches us the critical importance of bridging historical gaps and connecting past, present, and future. His efforts to unify the Nephite records with those of another group (the Mulekites) and his role in the migration narrative highlight the themes of unity and providence.

In sum, the lives and records of Amaron, Chemish, Abinadom, and Amaleki, though individually brief, collectively teach profound lessons about the roles of record keepers in preserving not just history but also the faith, culture, and divine interactions of their people. They remind us of our responsibility to document our times faithfully, preserve truth, and ensure continuity, all while engaging actively in the defense and development of our communities. These lessons resonate with anyone entrusted with cultural, historical, or spiritual legacies, challenging us to be diligent, faithful, and proactive in our stewardship.

Author's Reflection

In contemplating the lives of these diligent record keepers—
Enos, Jarom, Omni, and their successors—I am deeply moved by
their unwavering commitment to their sacred trust, a commitment
that challenges us today to approach our own responsibilities with
equal reverence and dedication. Their example challenges us in the
modern world to approach our own responsibilities with the same
reverence and dedication, ensuring that the legacies we inherit and
pass on are treated with the utmost care and respect. Their
dedication to maintaining these records not only safeguarded the
spiritual heritage of the Nephites but also ensured that future
generations could benefit from the teachings and experiences of
their forebears. Each character embodies distinct virtues—faith,
persistence, humility, and stewardship—that are essential for both
personal spiritual growth and the well-being of our communities.

Enos: A Model of Devotion and Prayerful Commitment

Enos, the son of Jacob, is best known for his powerful
experience with prayer as described in Enos 1:4-12. His journey
from seeking forgiveness for his own sins to praying for the welfare
of his people and even his enemies reveal a heart deeply committed
to God and to the well-being of others. Enos's faith and persistence

in prayer demonstrate a profound trust in God's ability to answer prayers and to provide spiritual guidance.

Reflecting on Enos's life, I see a model of faith and persistence that challenges us to deepen our own spiritual practices. Enos's extended prayer in the wilderness (Enos 1:4) illustrates the power of sincere and persistent communication with God. In our modern lives, Enos's example encourages us to cultivate a habit of earnest prayer, not just for ourselves but for the welfare of others, including those who may oppose us. His life teaches us that true faith is active, persistent, and deeply concerned with the spiritual and temporal well-being of the entire community.

Jarom: A Steward of Record and Righteousness

Jarom, the son of Enos, carries on the responsibility of maintaining the records and ensuring that the spiritual and temporal welfare of the Nephites is preserved. In his brief account, Jarom emphasizes the importance of keeping the commandments and the need for continued diligence in teaching and leading the people in righteousness (Jarom 1:5-7). His record, though concise, reflects a commitment to preserving the spiritual integrity of his people and ensuring that they remain faithful to the covenants made with God.

Jarom's life offers valuable lessons in stewardship, demonstrating how the faithful preservation of spiritual and moral integrity ensures continuity across generations. His emphasis on the continued teaching of the law and the protection of the people from falling into transgression (Jarom 1:10-12) serves as a reminder that spiritual vigilance is essential in every generation. In our modern context, Jarom's example challenges us to be diligent stewards of the spiritual and moral teachings we have received, ensuring that they are preserved and passed on to future generations. His life teaches us that maintaining the integrity of our spiritual heritage requires constant effort and dedication, both individually and communally.

Omni: A Link in the Chain of Nephite Record Keepers

Omni, the son of Jarom, contributes only a brief account to the record, acknowledging that he was not as faithful as his predecessors (Omni 1:2-3). However, his willingness to continue the record-keeping tradition despite his personal shortcomings demonstrates a sense of duty to his forebears and to future generations. Omni's candid admission of his failings, juxtaposed with his dedication to continuing the sacred record, offers a rare glimpse into the human struggles behind the preservation of divine history. His honesty adds a layer of authenticity to the records, reminding future generations that the divine narrative is carried forward by imperfect yet committed individuals.

Reflecting on Omni's life, I am reminded of the importance of persistence and humility (Omni 1:2) in fulfilling our responsibilities, particularly as part of a larger narrative that spans generations and shapes the spiritual future of our communities. In modern life, Omni's example encourages us to acknowledge our limitations while still striving to fulfill our duties to the best of our abilities. His life teaches us that even when we feel inadequate, our efforts to contribute to the well-being of our communities are valuable and necessary.

Amaron, Chemish, Abinadom, and Amaleki: Brief Stewards of a Sacred Legacy

The record keepers Amaron, Chemish, Abinadom, and Amaleki each add their brief accounts to the record, contributing to the preservation of the Nephite history and spiritual teachings. Amaron speaks of the increasing wickedness of the people and the mercy of the Lord in sparing the righteous (Omni 1:5-6). Chemish, in his single verse, acknowledges his responsibility to continue the record (Omni 1:9). Abinadom mentions the wars and contentions among the Nephites, while Amaleki provides a more detailed account, including the story of Mosiah and the merging of the Nephites with the people of Zarahemla (Omni 1:12-19).

These brief records, though not extensive, highlight the importance of each generation's contribution to the preservation of spiritual knowledge and historical context. The lives of these record keepers remind us that our contributions, however small, are part of a larger tapestry of faith and history. In modern contexts, their examples challenge us to recognize the value of our own contributions, no matter how seemingly insignificant. They teach us that by fulfilling our responsibilities, we help preserve the spiritual and moral foundations of our communities for future generations.

Summary

The characters of Chapter 5 Enos, Jarom, Omni, Amaron, Chemish, Abinadom, and Amaleki, each offer profound insights into the importance of faith, persistence, stewardship, and humility in preserving spiritual legacies. Their lives provide timeless lessons that are essential for both personal spiritual growth and the well-being of our communities, reminding us that the preservation of spiritual legacies is a collective effort that requires faith, diligence, and a deep sense of responsibility.

Enos teaches us the power of persistent prayer and the importance of interceding for others. Jarom emphasizes the need for continued spiritual vigilance and the diligent preservation of righteous teachings. Omni reminds us of the importance of fulfilling our duties even when we feel inadequate, and the collective record keepers Amaron, Chemish, Abinadom, and Amaleki highlight the value of each generation's contribution to the larger spiritual narrative.

As I reflect on these characters, I am inspired to cultivate these qualities in my own life. These ancient record keepers not only preserved the past; they laid a foundation for the future. As we strive to emulate their virtues: faith, persistence, humility, and stewardship, we too can contribute to a legacy that will inspire and guide future generations, ensuring that our communities remain anchored in principles of righteousness and faith.

Part III

Voices from the Past – Guidance

from the Plates of Brass

Part III delves into the profound influence of the ancient prophets whose writings, preserved on the Plates of Brass, provided essential guidance for the Nephite civilization. This section includes two chapters that examine how these voices from the past shaped the spiritual and doctrinal foundations of the Nephites. These chapters are included in Part III because they highlight the critical role these prophets played in guiding the Nephites, offering timeless principles and prophetic insights that helped maintain faith and navigate their spiritual journey.

Together, these two chapters illustrate the vital role the teachings preserved on the Plates of Brass played in the Nephite society. The words of the ancient prophets were not just historical records; they were a living source of divine wisdom that continued to instruct and inspire the Nephite people. By preserving these teachings, the Nephites ensured that the spiritual heritage of their ancestors continued to influence their lives, providing them with the guidance needed to understand divine purposes and maintain their covenant with God.

Chapter 6

Prophets and Kings of the Brass Plates

The Brass Plates, brought from Jerusalem by Lehi's family, contained the writings of ancient prophets who profoundly influenced Nephite theology and culture. This chapter delves into the lives and teachings of Zenock, Neum, Zenos—prophets, and King Zedekiah, whose prophecies and words provided spiritual guidance and doctrinal foundations for the Nephite people.

Historical Context

The Brass Plates, obtained by Nephi and his brothers from Laban in Jerusalem, were a significant repository of Jewish scripture and genealogy. These plates not only included the five books of Moses and a record of the Jews but also the writings of several prophets who were lesser-known in the traditional biblical canon but highly revered in Nephite culture. The preservation and study of these writings were crucial for maintaining the religious identity and continuity of Lehi's descendants in the New World. The teachings from the Brass Plates provided essential doctrinal foundations that shaped the spiritual journey of the Nephites, offering timeless principles that guided their understanding of divine purposes.

Characters in Chapter 6

- **Zenock** ~ A prophet whose writings on the Brass Plates emphasized the coming of the Messiah and His atonement, contributing significantly to Nephite messianic expectations.
- **Neum** ~ A prophet who prophesied the crucifixion of Christ, offering early and vital testimony of the Messiah's suffering and the redemptive plan.
- **Zenos** ~ Known for his allegories and parables, particularly the allegory of the olive tree, which powerfully illustrates

God's relationship with Israel and His ongoing efforts to nurture and save His people.

- **Zedekiah** ~ The last king of Judah before the Babylonian exile, whose reign and its tragic end provide historical context for the Brass Plates and underscore the consequences of ignoring prophetic counsel.

This historical context emphasizes the critical role the writings on the Brass Plates played in shaping the Nephite spiritual and doctrinal landscape. The teachings of Zenock, Neum, and Zenos provided a rich tapestry of messianic prophecy and theological insight that became central to Nephite religion. Understanding these prophets and their contributions helps us appreciate the continuity and depth of Nephite scriptural tradition, highlighting themes of atonement, divine mercy, and the ultimate redemption of God's people.

Zenock: A Prophet of Mercy and Atonement

Zenock, a prophet whose writings are found on the Plates of Brass and referenced in the Book of Mormon **(1 Nephi 19:10; 21)**, exemplifies several Christlike attributes, notably his profound understanding of God's mercy and the centrality of the Atonement. His teachings, as cited by Nephi, focus on the redemptive power of the Messiah and the necessity of faith and repentance. Zenock's prophecies highlight his deep commitment to God's plan of salvation and his compassion for the welfare of his people, demonstrating a heartfelt devotion to conveying the message of divine love and redemption.

Lessons and Teachings from Zenock's Life and Prophecies

Zenock's teachings, as preserved in the Book of Mormon, offer timeless lessons on divine justice, mercy, and the redemptive power of the Messiah.

Understanding Divine Mercy

Zenock's emphasis on the mercy of God, especially in his prophecy about the Atonement, underscores a profound theological insight—that the core of God's dealings with humanity is His mercy. Zenock's assertion that the Lord God would visit His people in His mercy (1 Nephi 19:10) reflects a deep understanding of God's compassionate nature and His desire to save rather than condemn. Reflecting on this teaching, we are reminded of the importance of recognizing and embracing God's mercy in our daily lives and extending that mercy to others.

The Centrality of the Atonement

Zenock's prophecies about the Atonement of Jesus Christ highlight the central role of this divine act in the plan of salvation. By focusing on the Atonement, Zenock teaches us about the profound love of God that underpins the sacrifice of His Son. This focus invites us to deepen our gratitude for this sacrifice and to live in a manner that honors this great gift, enhancing our commitment to Christlike living.

Faith and Repentance

Through his teachings, Zenock emphasizes the necessity of faith and repentance, key principles for those who wish to partake in the blessings of the Atonement. His prophecies serve as calls to action, urging us to turn from our sins and embrace the path of spiritual renewal. This emphasis on repentance and faith as essential components of spiritual life challenges us to examine our lives, identify areas needing change, and actively seek God's forgiveness and guidance.

Prophetic Courage and Integrity

Finally, Zenock's willingness to prophesy of Christ in what were likely hostile circumstances exemplifies prophetic courage and integrity. His steadfastness in proclaiming truths that may not have been popular or safe reminds us of the courage required to stand firm in our convictions, especially when faced with opposition or indifference.

In sum, Zenock, as a prophetic figure in the Book of Mormon, provides a rich legacy of teachings that resonate with the core themes of Christianity. His life and prophecies encourage us to embrace divine mercy, appreciate the central role of the Atonement in our spiritual journey, commit to a life of repentance and faith, and uphold our convictions with courage and integrity. Through his example, we learn the power of prophetic voice in shaping a life deeply connected to divine purposes and committed to conveying God's eternal truths.

Neum: A Witness of Christ's Atonement

Neum, although briefly mentioned in the Book of Mormon **(1 Nephi 19:10)**, is noted specifically for his prophecy regarding the crucifixion of Jesus Christ. His ability to foresee such a significant event highlights his profound spiritual insight and connection to divine revelation. Like other prophets in the scriptures, Neum's prophetic calling equipped him with the foresight to testify of Christ's mortal ministry and atoning sacrifice, reflecting a deep commitment to God's plan and a devotion to truth. Such attributes align closely with Christlike virtues of faith, hope, and charity, underscoring his role as a spiritual guide and visionary.

Lessons and Teachings from Neum's Prophecy

The prophecy of Neum about Christ's crucifixion, though succinct, offers significant lessons about prophecy, the nature of God's revelations, and the eternal impact of Christ's Atonement.

Prophecy as a Beacon of Hope and Warning

Neum's prophetic vision serves as both a beacon of hope and a stern warning. By foretelling the crucifixion of Christ, Neum highlights the central role of the Atonement in God's plan of salvation. This prophecy would have served to anchor the faith of those who looked forward to the Messiah's coming. Reflecting on this prophecy, we learn the dual role of prophetic messages to both warn of consequences and offer hope through divine intervention. It challenges us to consider how we respond to prophetic warnings and promises in our own lives.

Understanding the Nature of Divine Sacrifice

Neum's prophecy about Christ's crucifixion underscores the sacrificial nature of the Atonement. It prefigures the suffering Christ would endure to redeem mankind, illustrating the profound love and mercy of God. Reflecting on this, we can deepen our appreciation for the Savior's suffering and the purpose behind it, encouraging a more personal and profound commitment to Him. It invites us to contemplate the depth of God's love for us, prompting more heartfelt gratitude and a renewed dedication to live according to His commandments.

The Role of Prophets in Testifying of Christ

Neum, as a prophet, contributes to a larger tapestry of prophetic witness that consistently points to Jesus Christ. This example highlights the role of prophets not only as foretellers of future events but as essential testifiers of Christ's divine mission. Reflecting on Neum's contribution, we can appreciate the consistent and unified testimony of prophets across dispensations, which strengthens our own testimonies of Jesus Christ and His gospel.

In sum, although Neum's mention in the Book of Mormon is brief, the implications of his prophecy are profound, offering us insights into the nature of prophecy, the depth of the Atonement, and the enduring role of prophets in bearing witness of Christ. Through his teachings, we are reminded of the power of divine guidance through prophetic voices and the eternal significance of the sacrifices made by our Savior, Jesus Christ.

Zenos: A Prophet of the Vineyard and Divine Purposes

Zenos, a Hebrew prophet whose teachings are preserved in the Book of Mormon **(1 Nephi 19:10-16; Jacob 5:1)**, is particularly known for his allegory of the olive tree, which exemplifies profound Christlike attributes such as patience, foresight, and deep understanding of God's love and justice. Zenos's allegory and other prophecies reveal his deep spiritual insights into God's dealings with His children, emphasizing the Lord's persistent efforts to nourish, prune, and save His vineyard, which represents His people. Zenos's portrayal of God in the allegory reflects attributes of mercy, long-suffering, and tireless dedication to salvation—qualities that he, as a prophet, also embodied in his ministry.

Lessons and Teachings from Zenos's Life and Writings

Deep Understanding of Divine Love and Justice

The allegory of the olive tree, as taught by Zenos and recounted by Jacob in the Book of Mormon, provides rich insights into the nature of God's love and justice. The master of the vineyard, who represents God, shows both disappointment at the decay of the trees and a relentless commitment to their recovery. This allegory teaches us about God's balanced approach to justice—He is neither quick to condemn nor to overlook faults but rather works tirelessly to restore and heal. Reflecting on this, we learn the importance of balancing justice and mercy in our own lives, striving to emulate God's patience and persistent efforts in our dealings with others.

The Importance of Spiritual Nourishment and Pruning

Zenos's allegory also focuses on the necessary processes of nourishing and pruning the olive trees, symbolizing spiritual care and necessary corrections in our lives. Just as the master of the vineyard cuts off the dead branches and grafts into new ones, we too must continually assess our spiritual lives, embracing growth and cutting away habits or influences that stifle our spiritual progress. This imagery invites us to be active participants in our spiritual growth, embracing both the nourishing and pruning processes that God administers for our ultimate benefit.

Hope and Redemption for All

Zenos's teachings encompass a universal scope of salvation, indicating that all—Jew and Gentile—are part of God's plan for salvation. This inclusive perspective is especially highlighted in his prophecies about the gathering of Israel and the role of the Gentiles in this divine plan (1 Nephi 19:15-16). From this, we learn the lesson of universal compassion and inclusion, recognizing that God's love and salvation extend beyond cultural or religious boundaries. This calls us to expand our own circles of concern and outreach, embodying God's inclusive love in our interactions and ministries.

In sum, Zenos, as a voice from the ancient scriptures preserved by Nephite prophets, offers profound lessons on understanding divine attributes, participating in our spiritual development, and embracing a universal perspective on salvation. His teachings not only enrich our scriptural understanding but also challenge us to live lives that reflect divine patience, diligent spiritual stewardship, and inclusive love.

Zedekiah: A Case of Leadership and Its Trials

Zedekiah, the last king of Judah before the Babylonian captivity **(1 Nephi 1:4; Omni 15)**, presents a complex figure whose leadership and decisions provide lessons more in their flaws and outcomes than in exemplifying Christlike attributes. Zedekiah's reign was marked by political and spiritual instability, and his actions often reflected the struggles of a leader caught between external pressures and internal guidance. While Zedekiah himself may not have demonstrated many Christlike attributes, his story serves as a cautionary tale about the consequences of failing to adhere to prophetic warnings and divine commands.

Lessons and Teachings from Zedekiah's Life

The reign of Zedekiah provides critical lessons about leadership, the importance of heeding prophetic counsel, and the consequences of disobedience.

The Challenges of Leadership

Zedekiah's reign highlights the challenges faced by leaders who must balance external pressures with internal convictions. As a vassal of Babylon, Zedekiah was in a precarious position, needing to appease his overlords while managing the expectations and rebellious spirit of his people. This scenario underscores the complexities of leadership, especially when it lacks a firm grounding in ethical or spiritual principles. It invites current leaders to reflect on their sources of guidance and the foundations of their decision-making processes.

The Consequences of Ignoring Prophetic Counsel

Zedekiah's failure to heed the warnings of Jeremiah, who represented the voice of divine wisdom, ultimately led to catastrophic results for Judah. This aspect of his reign teaches the critical importance of listening to and acting upon prophetic guidance. In the modern context, it serves as a reminder of the value of spiritual and moral guidance in governing and personal decision-making.

The Importance of Moral Integrity in Leadership

Zedekiah's inability to assert moral leadership, swayed as he was by the nobles and his fear of Babylon, highlights the importance of moral integrity and courage in leadership roles. His story is a cautionary tale about the perils of moral compromise and the lack of personal conviction. Reflecting on this, individuals and leaders alike can learn about the crucial role of steadfast principles and ethical consistency in ensuring righteous and effective leadership.

Divine Justice and Mercy

Lastly, Zedekiah's story, while predominantly tragic, also touches on themes of divine justice and the potential for mercy. The destruction of Jerusalem, though a severe punishment, was also a mechanism for eventual renewal and return, as later prophesied and realized in the scriptures. This teaches that divine justice, while often severe, also aims toward correction and ultimate good.

In sum, King Zedekiah's reign, as reflected upon in the Book of Mormon, offers sobering lessons on the responsibilities of leadership and the grave consequences of ignoring divine counsel. His story encourages a deep consideration of our actions, urging a leadership style that is both morally grounded and responsive to wise counsel.

Author's Reflection

As I reflect on the lives of Zenock, Neum, Zenos, and Zedekiah, I am struck by the enduring power of their prophetic teachings and the profound faith that characterized their ministries. These prophets, whose voices echo through the scriptures, provide timeless guidance not only for the ancient Israelites but also for us today as we navigate our own spiritual journeys. Each prophet offers unique insights into the nature of divine guidance, the role of prophecy, and the importance of faith in achieving both personal and communal promised lands.

Zenock: Lessons from a Prophet of the Atonement

Zenock is mentioned in the Book of Mormon as a prophet who testified of Christ and was persecuted for his teachings (Alma 33:15-17). His teachings on the Atonement, particularly his emphasis on the necessity of faith in the coming Messiah, highlight his deep understanding of God's redemptive plan. Zenock's willingness to speak the truth despite opposition reflects a profound commitment to his divine calling and an unshakeable faith in God's promises.

Reflecting on Zenock's life, I see a powerful example of courage and conviction. His teachings remind us that faith in the Atonement of Christ is central to our spiritual journey and that this faith can sustain us through trials and opposition. In our modern lives, Zenock's example challenges us to stand firm in our beliefs, even when they are unpopular or met with resistance. His life teaches us that true faith is not passive but requires active testimony and a willingness to endure persecution for the sake of truth. As we seek our own promised lands—whether they be spiritual goals, personal growth, or community prosperity—Zenock's life reminds us that the Atonement of Christ is the foundation upon which all true progress is built.

Neum: A Witness of Christ's Atonement

Neum is another prophet mentioned in the Book of Mormon who prophesied of Christ's crucifixion (1 Nephi 19:10). Though we know little about his life, Neum's prophecy is significant for its clear and direct testimony of the Savior's sacrifice. His teachings reflect a deep awareness of the importance of Christ's suffering and death as central to God's plan for the redemption of humanity.

Reflecting on Neum's life and teachings, I am reminded of the importance of recognizing and testifying of the central truths of the gospel. Neum's prophecy of Christ's crucifixion highlights the need for us to understand and appreciate the profound significance of the Atonement in our lives. In modern contexts, Neum's example challenges us to focus on the core principles of the gospel and to bear witness to these truths to others. His life teaches us that the

Atonement is not just a historical event but the key to understanding our purpose and potential in this life and the life to come. As we journey toward our own promised lands, Neum's testimony encourages us to keep the Atonement at the center of our faith, guiding our actions and shaping our character.

Zenos: A Prophet of the Vineyard and Divine Purposes

Zenos is one of the most prominent prophets in the Book of Mormon, known for his allegory of the olive tree found in Jacob 5. This allegory, which describes the scattering and gathering of Israel, illustrates God's enduring patience and efforts to nurture and reclaim His people. Zenos's teachings are rich with symbolism and insight into the nature of God's dealings with humanity, emphasizing themes of mercy, judgment, and divine intervention.

Reflecting on Zenos's life and teachings, I see a profound lesson in the patience and long-suffering nature of God. The allegory of the olive tree teaches us about the ongoing process of spiritual growth, repentance, and redemption. It reminds us that God is constantly working in our lives, pruning, grafting, and nurturing us to help us reach our full potential. In modern life, Zenos's allegory challenges us to be patient with ourselves and others as we journey toward our promised lands. It teaches us that spiritual growth is a process that requires time, effort, and divine intervention. Zenos's life also encourages us to recognize God's hand in the events of our lives, trusting that His purposes are being fulfilled even when the path is difficult or unclear.

Zedekiah: A Case of Leadership and Its Trials

Zedekiah, the last king of Judah, is mentioned in the Book of Mormon as the father of Mulek, who fled to the Americas after the fall of Jerusalem (Helaman 8:21). Zedekiah's reign was marked by political turmoil, rebellion against Babylon, and ultimately the destruction of Jerusalem. While his leadership was fraught with challenges and his decisions led to significant consequences for his people, the mention of Zedekiah in the Book of Mormon underscores the far-reaching impact of leadership, both for good and ill.

Reflecting on Zedekiah's life, I am reminded of the heavy responsibility that comes with leadership and the profound impact that leaders can have on the course of history. Zedekiah's choices, particularly his decision to rebel against Babylon despite prophetic counsel to the contrary (Jeremiah 27:12), serve as a cautionary tale about the dangers of pride and the consequences of disregarding divine guidance. In modern contexts, Zedekiah's life challenges leaders to carefully consider the long-term implications of their decisions and to seek divine counsel in times of crisis. His life teaches us that leadership requires humility, wisdom, and a willingness to follow God's direction, even when it is difficult. As we navigate our own roles as leaders in our families, communities, and organizations, Zedekiah's story reminds us of the importance of aligning our decisions with God's will to ensure that we lead others toward, rather than away from, their promised lands.

Summary

The characters of Chapter 6 Zenock, Neum, Zenos, and Zedekiah each offer profound insights into the principles of faith, prophecy, leadership, and divine guidance. Their lives provide timeless lessons that are essential for our personal spiritual growth and for the well-being of our communities as we seek to achieve our own promised lands.

Zenock teaches us the importance of courage and conviction in bearing testimony of the Atonement, even in the face of opposition. Neum reminds us to focus on the central truths of the gospel and to bear witness of Christ's sacrifice. Zenos's allegory of the olive tree provides a powerful lesson in the patience and ongoing work of God in our lives, encouraging us to trust in His divine purposes. Zedekiah's life serves as a reminder of the responsibilities of leadership and the importance of humility and divine guidance in decision-making.

As I reflect on these prophets, I am inspired to cultivate these qualities in my own life. Their teachings challenge us to remain steadfast in our faith, to bear testimony of the truths we know, and to trust in God's guidance as we journey toward our own promised lands. Whether in our personal lives, our families, or our communities, the examples of Zenock, Neum, Zenos, and Zedekiah remind us that our ultimate success in reaching our promised lands depends on our willingness to follow divine guidance, to lead with humility, and to nurture the spiritual growth of ourselves and others.

Chapter 7

Major Prophets and Their Teachings

The inclusion of these prophets in the Brass Plates underscores the universality of their messages, which extend beyond the Nephites to all of God's covenant people, offering timeless principles for maintaining faith, obedience, and spiritual integrity. This chapter explores the contributions of Isaiah, Jeremiah, Moses, and Joseph (the son of Jacob), whose prophecies and writings provided doctrinal foundations and spiritual guidance for the Nephite people. Understanding their teachings offers profound insights into the continuity of God's revelations and the enduring principles that guided the Nephites.

Historical Context

The Brass Plates, which were essential to the spiritual heritage of Lehi's family, included not only genealogical records and the five books of Moses but also the writings of major prophets. These records were integral to maintaining the religious identity and doctrinal purity of the Nephite civilization in the New World. The inclusion of these prophetic writings underscored not only the Nephites' connection to their Israelite heritage but also the continuity of divine revelation, demonstrating how God's guidance extends across generations to His covenant people.

Characters in Chapter 7

- **Isaiah** ~ His teachings on repentance and redemption not only shaped Nephite theology but continue to offer timeless guidance on maintaining faith in divine promises.
- **Jeremiah** ~ His urgent calls for repentance remind us of the importance of heeding spiritual warnings in our own lives.
- **Moses** ~ His role as lawgiver provides a foundation for understanding the balance between divine law and grace.
- **Joseph (son of Jacob)** ~ His story of perseverance and divine providence encourages us to trust in God's plan, even in the face of adversity.

This historical context highlights the significance of the major prophets whose writings were included in the Brass Plates. Their teachings provided essential doctrinal foundations and spiritual guidance that shaped the Nephite civilization. Understanding the contributions of Isaiah, Jeremiah, Moses, and Joseph helps us appreciate the continuity of God's revelations and the enduring principles of faith, obedience, and divine providence that guided the Nephite people. These prophets not only linked the Nephites to their Israelite heritage but also provided timeless lessons on repentance, redemption, and the ultimate fulfillment of God's promises.

Isaiah: A Prophet of Redemption and Vision

Isaiah, one of the most quoted prophets in the Book of Mormon **(1 Nephi 19:23-24) (2 Nephi 6:5; 25:1-4)**, exemplifies several Christlike attributes through his profound prophecies and poetic writings. His deep spiritual insight, commitment to truth, and visionary foresight are evident throughout his teachings. Isaiah's ability to foresee the coming of the Messiah and vividly describe the Savior's life and atonement centuries before they occurred highlights his prophetic gift and his deep connection to divine inspiration. His messages often blend warnings of judgment with promises of hope and redemption, reflecting a balance of justice and mercy characteristic of Christlike empathy and compassion.

Lessons and Teachings from Isaiah's Life

Isaiah's prophecies not only looked forward to the coming of Christ but were also fulfilled in Him, demonstrating the accuracy and depth of Isaiah's spiritual insight. For believers, Isaiah's visions provide a roadmap for recognizing and understanding Christ's role as Redeemer and King. His writings, interwoven into the Nephite narrative, enrich our understanding of God's dealings with His children and the eternal principles of righteousness.

Visionary Leadership

Isaiah's ability to see beyond the immediate crises of his time to a future of redemption and divine kingship is a hallmark of visionary leadership. His prophecies about the coming of Christ, the establishment of Zion, and the gathering of Israel provide hope and direction not only to his contemporaries but to all future generations who read his words. This forward-looking perspective teaches the importance of visionary leadership in guiding people through present challenges with an eye toward future redemption.

Empathy and Compassion in Prophetic Warnings

Although Isaiah's messages often contain stern warnings about the consequences of sin and rebellion, they are also replete with expressions of God's love and promises of restoration for those who repent. This duality reflects a Christlike empathy—Isaiah, like Christ, weeps for the sins of the people but also rejoices in their potential for salvation (Isaiah 22:4; 62:5). Reflecting on Isaiah's approach prompts me to consider how balance between truth and love is essential in effective communication, especially when addressing difficult truths.

Enduring Faith in God's Promises

Isaiah's steadfast proclamation of God's promises, despite the dire circumstances of his time, underscores the importance of enduring faith. His famous declaration, "Though the mountains depart, and the hills be removed, yet my kindness shall not depart from thee" (Isaiah 54:10), offers profound assurance of God's unwavering commitment to His people. This teaches us the power of holding fast to faith in God's promises, even when current events seem overwhelming or discouraging.

In sum, Isaiah's teachings and life offer rich insights into dealing with adversity, maintaining hope, and understanding the divine plan of salvation. Isaiah's prophecies of hope and redemption are particularly relevant in times of global uncertainty and personal trials. His forward-looking vision invites us to anchor our faith in the promised future of divine intervention and ultimate peace, encouraging resilience and trust in God's plan amid the challenges we face today.

Jeremiah: A Prophet of Conscience and Courage

Jeremiah, known as the "weeping prophet," **(1 Nephi 6:13, 7:14)** exemplifies several Christlike attributes, notably his unwavering commitment to truth, profound compassion, and immense courage in the face of adversity. Jeremiah's ministry is marked by his relentless call for repentance to the people of Judah and his poignant laments over their sins and the impending destruction of Jerusalem. His ability to empathize deeply with both the divine sorrow and the suffering of his people reflects a profound spiritual depth and emotional intelligence, mirroring the empathy Christ showed during His earthly ministry.

Jeremiah also demonstrates great personal integrity and bravery. He delivers unpopular prophecies despite intense persecution, including threats to his life, imprisonment, and public humiliation. His steadfastness in proclaiming God's messages, despite the personal cost, aligns closely with Christ's attribute of staying true to His mission regardless of opposition.

Lessons and Teachings from Jeremiah's Life

Jeremiah's sufferings were not merely personal trials but were integral to his prophetic witness. His life challenges us to see suffering as a potential vehicle for divine action, teaching us about the redemptive possibilities within our own hardships.

The Cost of Prophetic Ministry

Jeremiah's experiences underscore the reality that being a spokesperson for God often involves significant personal sacrifices. His life exemplifies the cost of discipleship—standing for truth can lead to persecution, but it also leads to spiritual integrity and divine approval. Jeremiah's persistence invites us to reflect on our commitment to truth and righteousness, asking us to consider what we are willing to endure for the sake of being faithful to God's call.

Compassion Amidst Judgment

Throughout his prophecies, Jeremiah expresses a deep compassion for his people, despite their rebellion against God. His laments, particularly seen in chapters such as Jeremiah 9 and 31, reveal a heart that is profoundly aligned with God's love and sorrow over human sin. This balance of justice and mercy in his ministry teaches us about the nature of godly leadership, which must always be tempered with compassion and hope for redemption.

The Role of Suffering in Divine Providence

Jeremiah's personal sufferings—ranging from being thrown into a cistern to being publicly humiliated—are not just trials but also part of his prophetic witness to the people. His sufferings parallel the sufferings of Christ in many ways, underscoring the theme that suffering can be redemptive and purposeful when it is endured in faithfulness to God's will. Reflecting on Jeremiah's life challenges us to view our sufferings through the lens of what God might be accomplishing through them, both in us and in those around us.

In sum, Jeremiah's unwavering moral courage serves as a model for modern-day prophets and leaders who must navigate the complexities of truth-telling in a world often resistant to divine guidance. His life challenges contemporary leaders to stand firm in their convictions, embodying the balance of compassion and justice in their ministry.

Moses: A Paradigm of Prophetic Leadership and Deliverance

Moses is revered in the Book of Mormon **(1 Nephi 4:2, 17:29)** **(2 Nephi 3:10, 17)** not only as a great prophet but also as a powerful exemplar of several Christlike attributes, particularly those of faith, leadership, perseverance, and advocacy for his people. As a deliverer of the Israelites from Egyptian bondage, Moses embodies faith and obedience to God's commands, often facing immense challenges and opposition with courage and steadfastness. His interactions with God, particularly at pivotal moments like the parting of the Red Sea and receiving the tablets of the law on Mount Sinai, demonstrate his deep connection to divine guidance and his role as a mediator between God and his people.

Furthermore, Moses' patience and long-suffering are profound, as he leads a frequently murmuring and disobedient people through the wilderness for forty years. His life reflects a profound commitment to God's purposes and a compassionate, albeit sometimes strained, dedication to his role as a leader and shepherd to a wayward flock, mirroring Christ's role as the Good Shepherd.

Lessons and Teachings from Moses' Life

Moses' role as a mediator between God and Israel prefigures Christ's role as the ultimate Mediator of the new covenant. His giving of the Law to Israel sets the stage for understanding Christ's fulfillment and expansion of the Law in the New Testament, offering believers a deeper appreciation of divine law and grace.

Leadership and Advocacy

Moses' leadership is characterized by his relentless advocacy for his people, even in the face of their frequent transgressions. His willingness to intercede for the Israelites, asking God to spare them after the incident with the golden calf (Exodus 32), showcases a leader's responsibility towards his people. This aspect of Moses' character challenges us to consider the qualities of true leadership—how a leader must sometimes bear the burden of advocacy in interceding for others, a trait deeply resonant with Christ's atoning sacrifice.

Faith in Divine Commands

Moses' life is a testament to the power of faith in action. His obedience to God's commands, often under seemingly impossible circumstances, such as confronting Pharaoh or leading his people through the Red Sea, highlights the importance of unwavering faith and trust in divine promises. This teaches us about the necessity of faith when we face our own 'Red Seas' and 'Pharaohs'—the seemingly insurmountable challenges in our lives.

Perseverance Through Trials

Moses' journey through the wilderness with a murmuring and often disobedient people exemplifies perseverance. His ability to continue leading, teaching, and staying faithful to God throughout these trials provides a powerful example for enduring our spiritual journeys. This aspect of Moses' story invites reflection on our patience and fortitude in spiritual commitments and leadership roles.

In sum, Moses' leadership, characterized by humility, perseverance, and advocacy, provides a timeless template for modern spiritual and temporal leaders. His example teaches us that true leadership involves guiding others through transformative experiences with compassion, patience, and a deep reliance on divine guidance, especially in times of collective challenge. Reflecting on Moses' story encourages us to cultivate these same virtues in our lives, striving to emulate his faithfulness and commitment in our spiritual pursuits and leadership roles.

Joseph: A Model of Forgiveness and Divine Providence

Joseph, the son of Jacob and Rachel **(1 Nephi 5:14-16) (2 Nephi 3, 4)**, is revered not only for his remarkable life journey from slavery to prominence in Egypt but also for his profound display of forgiveness and foresight. These Christlike attributes are vividly evident throughout his life's story. Joseph's ability to forgive his brothers after they sold him into slavery—choosing reconciliation over retribution—mirrors the forgiving nature of Christ. Moreover, Joseph's insight and wisdom, which allowed him to interpret dreams and effectively manage Egypt's resources during famine, reflect divine guidance and providence.

Lessons and Teachings from Joseph's Life

Joseph's ability to discern God's purpose in his suffering offers a profound model for understanding divine providence in our own lives. His life teaches us to view our challenges through the lens of faith, trusting that God can bring about good even in the midst of adversity.

Forgiveness and Reconciliation

Perhaps the most profound lesson from Joseph's life is his ability to forgive those who wronged him severely. After rising to power in Egypt, Joseph encounters his brothers, who had sold him into slavery. Instead of seeking vengeance, he forgives them, recognizing that their actions, though intended for harm, were used by God to preserve many lives (Genesis 50:20). This act of forgiveness is a powerful example of seeing beyond personal pain to the broader purposes of God's plans. It challenges us to forgive others, not because they necessarily deserve it, but because forgiveness can fulfill divine purposes and lead to greater healing and reconciliation.

Wisdom and Providence in Leadership

Joseph's adept handling of Egypt's economic resources before and during a famine demonstrates his exceptional leadership and administrative skills, guided by divine insight. His ability to interpret Pharaoh's dreams and his subsequent strategies to store and manage grain reserves illustrate the importance of wisdom and preparation in leadership. This aspect of his life encourages us to seek divine guidance in our decision-making processes, particularly in roles that impact others' well-being.

Resilience and Faith in Trials

Joseph's journey from a pit to the palace is marked by several trials—from slavery and imprisonment to his ultimate rise to authority. Throughout these challenges, Joseph's faith in God remains unshaken. His resilience teaches us about the power of steadfast faith and trust in God's timing, even when our current circumstances seem dire or unjust.

In sum, Joseph's life, as reflected upon in the Book of Mormon and the Bible, provides timeless lessons in dealing with adversity, practicing forgiveness, and leading with integrity. Joseph's story inspires us to view our personal struggles as part of a broader divine plan, encouraging us to find purpose and meaning in adversity. His life serves as a blueprint for embracing forgiveness, recognizing divine providence in all circumstances, and trusting that even our deepest trials can lead to unforeseen blessings and opportunities.

Author's Reflection

In our modern world, the challenges faced by Isaiah, Jeremiah, Moses, and Joseph are mirrored in our own struggles with faith, leadership, and the pursuit of righteousness. These prophets remind us that the principles of divine guidance, forgiveness, and perseverance are as relevant today as they were in ancient times, offering us timeless wisdom for navigating the complexities of modern life. These figures stand as towering examples of faith, vision, and the enduring power of divine leadership. Each prophet's life and teachings offer unique insights into the challenges and rewards of spiritual leadership, the nature of divine covenants, and the importance of maintaining faith through trials. Their stories are as relevant today as they were in ancient times, guiding us as we seek to navigate our own paths to promised lands—both literal and figurative.

Isaiah: A Prophet of Redemption and Vision

Isaiah is one of the most quoted prophets in the Book of Mormon, revered for his profound visions of Christ's mission and the redemption of Israel. His prophecies are characterized by their poetic depth, spiritual insight, and far-reaching scope. Isaiah speaks of the gathering of Israel, the coming of the Messiah, and the ultimate triumph of God's kingdom (Isaiah 2:2-4; Isaiah 53). His teachings emphasize the need for repentance, faith, and the hope that comes from the assurance of God's promises.

Reflecting on Isaiah's life, I am inspired by his unwavering commitment to proclaiming God's message, even in the face of widespread rejection and opposition. Isaiah's vision of a future Zion (Isaiah 2:2-3) challenges us to look beyond the immediate difficulties we face and to focus on the ultimate fulfillment of God's promises. In our modern lives, Isaiah's example encourages us to maintain a long-term perspective, understanding that our journey to the promised land—whether spiritual or temporal—is part of a much larger divine plan. His prophecies remind us that faith in Christ and adherence to divine principles are the keys to achieving redemption and realizing the full potential of our personal and communal lives.

Jeremiah: A Prophet of Conscience and Courage

Jeremiah, known as the "weeping prophet," is a figure of immense moral courage and deep personal suffering. His ministry was marked by his unwavering commitment to delivering God's message of impending judgment to a nation that had largely turned away from righteousness. Despite the persecution he faced, including imprisonment and threats to his life (Jeremiah 20:2; Jeremiah 38:6), Jeremiah remained steadfast in his mission, *warning of the Babylonian captivity and calling the people to repentance (Jeremiah 7:1-15).*

Reflecting on Jeremiah's life, I see a powerful example of the cost of true discipleship and the courage required to stand up for truth, even when it is unpopular or dangerous. Jeremiah's life teaches us that faithfulness to God's commandments often requires great personal sacrifice, but it also brings the assurance of divine support and ultimate vindication. In our modern context, Jeremiah's example challenges us to be voices of conscience in our own communities, advocating for justice, righteousness, and repentance, even when it may lead to personal hardship. His story reminds us that the journey to our promised lands may be fraught with trials, but steadfast faith and obedience to God's will are the surest paths to spiritual and communal redemption.

Moses: A Paradigm of Prophetic Leadership and Deliverance

Moses is one of the most pivotal figures in the scriptures, leading the Israelites out of Egyptian bondage and guiding them through the wilderness toward the promised land. His life is a study in prophetic leadership, characterized by his deep humility (Numbers 12:3), his close relationship with God (Exodus 33:11), and his unwavering commitment to his people despite their frequent rebellions (Exodus 32:19; Numbers 14:11-19). Moses's role as lawgiver, intercessor, and guide is central to the spiritual and temporal formation of Israel as a covenant people.

Reflecting on Moses's life, I am reminded of the immense responsibilities that come with leadership and the profound trust in God that is required to fulfill such a role. Moses's life teaches us about the importance of perseverance, even in the face of seemingly insurmountable challenges. His leadership during the Exodus (Exodus 12:37-42) and his ability to mediate between God and the people highlight the vital role of spiritual leadership in guiding communities through periods of transformation. In modern life, Moses's example encourages us to lead with humility, to seek God's guidance in all things, and to remain committed to the well-being of those we serve, even when the journey is long and difficult. His life also reminds us that the journey to our promised lands often involves overcoming significant obstacles, but with faith and divine guidance, these challenges can be transformed into opportunities for growth and spiritual renewal.

Joseph: A Model of Forgiveness and Divine Providence

Joseph, the son of Jacob, is a figure whose life is marked by betrayal, suffering, and ultimately triumph through divine providence. Sold into slavery by his brothers, Joseph rises to become the second most powerful man in Egypt, where he saves his family and countless others from famine (Genesis 41:39-45; Genesis 45:5-8). Joseph's story is one of resilience, forgiveness, and the belief that God can bring good out of even the direst circumstances.

Reflecting on Joseph's life, I see a profound lesson in the power of forgiveness and the importance of trusting in God's plan, even when it is difficult to understand. Joseph's ability to forgive his brothers and recognize God's hand in his life (Genesis 50:20) teaches us about the importance of letting go of past grievances and embracing the opportunities that God places before us. In modern contexts, Joseph's story challenges us to see the trials and setbacks we face as part of a larger divine plan, trusting that God can use our experiences for good. His life encourages us to cultivate a spirit of forgiveness and to maintain faith in God's providence, even when the path to our promised lands seems fraught with difficulty and uncertainty.

Summary

As the Nephites preserved these teachings through the Brass Plates, we too are called to preserve and apply these prophetic insights in our own lives and communities. The timeless wisdom of Isaiah, Jeremiah, Moses, and Joseph guides us in navigating the complexities of modern life, encouraging us to uphold the principles of faith, leadership, and divine providence as we journey toward our own promised lands.

Isaiah challenges us to maintain a long-term perspective, focusing on the ultimate fulfillment of God's promises and the redemption that comes through Christ. Jeremiah teaches us the cost of true discipleship and the courage required to stand up for truth and righteousness, even in the face of persecution. Moses exemplifies prophetic leadership, showing us the importance of humility, perseverance, and divine guidance in leading others through transformative experiences. Joseph's life is a powerful testament to the importance of forgiveness and the belief in divine providence, encouraging us to trust in God's plan even in the midst of trials.

As I reflect on these prophets, I am inspired to cultivate these qualities in my own life. The Brass Plates preserved the teachings of these major prophets, ensuring that the Nephites and we today can draw from the deep well of divine wisdom they offer. The lives and teachings of Isaiah, Jeremiah, Moses, and Joseph not only shaped the spiritual journey of the Nephites but also offered enduring lessons for future generations. As we draw from the deep well of divine wisdom they provide, we are reminded that these principles of faith, leadership, and divine providence are essential for guiding us and those who follow us on the path to our promised lands.

Part IV

Jesus Christ and His Witnesses —

The Divine Center

The testimonies of Jesus Christ's witnesses were instrumental in solidifying Nephite faith, offering a clear understanding of Jesus Christ's role in salvation. These testimonies affirmed Jesus Christ's divine mission and provided the Nephites with a profound sense of purpose in their spiritual journey.

Building on the historical and doctrinal foundations laid in the previous sections, Part IV turns our attention to the ultimate purpose of Nephite teachings—the central role of Jesus Christ in their theology and the powerful testimonies of those who bore witness of His divine mission. For the Nephites, recognizing Jesus Christ as the divine center was more than doctrinal acknowledgment; it was the fulfillment of their covenant with God. This recognition profoundly influenced every aspect of their religious life, from temple worship to daily interactions, guiding their commitment to covenantal living.

The testimonies of Jesus Christ's witnesses were more than just affirmations of His divinity; they were foundational to the Nephite understanding of the gospel. These witnesses, through their inspired words and personal experiences, provided powerful confirmation of Jesus Christ's divine mission. Nephite leaders often relied on these testimonies to teach and reinforce the principles of the gospel, ensuring that each generation remained anchored in the truth of Christ's redemptive work. The centrality of Jesus Christ in Nephite theology was intrinsically linked to their understanding of salvation. To the Nephites, Jesus Christ's mission was the ultimate fulfillment of God's covenant with His people. It was a divine promise that through Jesus Christ, all would have the opportunity to receive salvation and eternal life. These testimonies not only shaped the faith of the Nephites but continue to offer timeless insights for believers today, reinforcing the centrality of Jesus Christ in our own spiritual journeys and guiding us toward salvation through His atoning sacrifice.

In the chapters that follow, we will explore the pivotal testimonies of Jesus Christ's key witnesses, including those divinely chosen to herald His coming and those who intimately knew Him. Each testimony uniquely contributed to the Nephite understanding of Jesus Christ's divine mission, serving as a guiding light that reinforced their faith and deepened their commitment to God's plan for salvation. These upcoming chapters will deepen our understanding of how these sacred testimonies continue to inspire and guide us in our quest for spiritual truth and salvation.

Chapter 8

The Messiah and His Herald

Central to the Nephite faith and the teachings recorded in the Book of Mormon are the prophecies and revelations concerning Jesus Christ, the Holy One of Israel. This chapter explores the roles and contributions of Jesus Christ and John the Revelator, whose prophecies and witness form the cornerstone of Nephite theology. Understanding their significance provides deep insights into the divine mission of Christ and the prophetic witness that heralds His coming.

Historical Context

The Nephite civilization, from its inception, was profoundly centered on the prophecies and expectations of the coming Messiah. The Brass Plates, brought from Jerusalem, contained numerous prophecies about Jesus Christ, which were elaborated upon by Nephite prophets. These prophecies not only reinforced the spiritual identity of the Nephites but also provided hope and direction amidst their trials and challenges. The Nephite prophets meticulously preserved and expounded upon these teachings in their records, ensuring that future generations would remain anchored in the truths of Jesus Christ's mission and John's prophetic witness, thereby reinforcing the covenantal relationship between God and His people.

Characters in Chapter 8

- **Jesus Christ** ~ The Holy One of Israel, whose life, atonement, and resurrection are the central themes of Nephite prophecy and theology.
- **John the Revelator** ~ Apostle and prophet whose apocalyptic visions provided a powerful witness of Christ's divinity and the ultimate fulfillment of God's plan.

Jesus Christ, the Redeemer, is central to the Nephite understanding of salvation, while John the Revelator serves as the prophetic witness whose visions confirm Christ's divine mission and foretell His ultimate triumph. This historical context emphasizes the centrality of Jesus Christ and the importance of prophetic witnesses like John the Revelator in Nephite theology. Their teachings and revelations form the bedrock of the Nephite faith, offering profound insights into the nature of Christ's mission and the unfolding of divine prophecy. Understanding the contributions of Jesus Christ and John the Revelator helps us appreciate the depth of Nephite spiritual understanding and their unwavering faith in the Savior's redemptive power. These teachings continue to inspire and guide believers, reinforcing the timeless message of salvation through Jesus Christ.

Jesus Christ: The Exemplar of Divine Love and Redemption

Jesus Christ, the central figure of Christianity and a pivotal figure in the Book of Mormon **(1 Nephi 10:4; 11:18; 2 Nephi 25:29)**, exemplifies the epitome of divine attributes, including unconditional love, infinite compassion, perfect humility, and supreme sacrifice. His life and ministry, as prophesied and revered in the Book of Mormon, demonstrate His role as the Savior and Redeemer of the world. His actions consistently reflect divine love—He heals the sick, teaches the pure doctrine, forgives sinners, and ultimately sacrifices His life for humanity's sins, embodying perfect obedience to the Father's will.

Lessons and Teachings from Jesus Christ's Life in the Small Plates of Nephi

The life and teachings of Jesus Christ, as anticipated in the Book of Mormon, offer profound lessons on the nature of divine love, the importance of obedience, and the power of atonement.

Divine Love and Compassion

Jesus's ministry is marked by acts of profound compassion and love. His willingness to heal the sick, bless the children, and comfort the afflicted demonstrates a love that is both divine and actionable (3 Nephi 17). This aspect of His life teaches us the importance of extending compassion and kindness to others, reflecting His love through our actions.

Perfect Example of Obedience

Jesus's life is the ultimate example of obedience to God's will. From His submission in Gethsemane to His last moments on the cross, where He declares, "It is finished" (John 19:30), Jesus fulfills the will of the Father completely. This teaches us about the nature of true obedience—not as a burden but as a willing submission to divine will, knowing that God's plans are greater than our own.

The Power of Atonement

Central to Jesus's teachings in the Book of Mormon is the doctrine of the Atonement. This infinite sacrifice is not only a central theme but is the pivotal event upon which all human salvation hinges. He invites all to come unto Him and partake of His goodness, emphasizing that through His suffering, all might be saved if they obey His commandments (2 Nephi 25:29). This profound truth underscores the accessibility of Christ's grace and the personal response required to access its power—repentance and obedience.

Enduring Faith and Hope

Jesus Christ embodies the virtues of faith and hope, not only during His earthly ministry but also in His promises regarding the latter days. His assurances of peace, His prophesied Second Coming, and His reign of millennial glory offer hope in a troubled world, encouraging us to remain steadfast in our faith and to look forward with joy to His promises (2 Nephi 30:5).

In sum, Jesus Christ's teachings and example, as presented in the Small Plates of Nephi in the Book of Mormon, illuminate His divine attributes and mission, providing a blueprint for how we should live our lives. His perfect example of love, obedience, sacrifice, and hope invites us to deepen our discipleship, enhance our capacity for compassion, and strengthen our commitment to follow Him. Through studying His life and applying His teachings, we not only come closer to Him but also advance in our own spiritual journey toward eternal life.

Following the divine example set by Jesus Christ, John the Revelator's writings serve as a beacon, illuminating the path laid out by the Savior. His role as a witness to Christ's divinity and as a prophet of the last days complements and expands the Nephite understanding of the Savior's mission.

John: Apostle of Testimony and Vision

John the Apostle, known for his deep spirituality and closeness to Jesus Christ **(1 Nephi 14:20-27)**, is celebrated for his profound insights into the nature of God and the eternal gospel. His Christlike attributes include a steadfast faith, fervent love, and visionary prophetic gifts. John's writings, especially his Gospel, three epistles, and the Book of Revelation, highlight his deep understanding of divine love ("God is love" - 1 John 4:8) and his commitment to sharing this transformative message with the world. In the Book of Mormon, John is mentioned in Nephi's vision as a future witness of Christ, described as one who would write concerning the end of the world, underscoring his role in expounding eschatological truths.

In the context of the Book of Mormon, Nephi's prophetic glimpse into the future acknowledges John's critical role in the Christian faith, particularly highlighting his responsibility to write concerning the last days and the fullness of the gospel of the Messiah. This prophetic endorsement reinforces John's authority and the enduring relevance of his writings.

Lessons and Teachings from John's Life

John's writings not only confirm Jesus Christ's divine mission but also offer a prophetic lens through which the Nephites and all believers can understand the ultimate victory of God's kingdom, reinforcing the hope and endurance necessary in the face of trials.

Profound Understanding of Divine Love

John's emphasis on love as the core of Christian life is both revolutionary and foundational. His assertion that love is from God and that knowing God is to love (1 John 4:7-8) challenges us to consider the depth of our own love for God and for each other. This teaching compels us to reflect on how love manifests in our daily actions and decisions, urging a lifestyle that actively demonstrates love through compassion, forgiveness, and service.

The Role of Personal Witness

John's firsthand experiences with Christ, his vivid recounting of the life, death, and resurrection of Jesus, and his bold testimony in the face of persecution exemplify the power of personal witness. As he declares, "That which was from the beginning, which we have heard, which we have seen with our eyes... and our hands have handled, of the Word of life" (1 John 1:1), he invites every believer to consider the authenticity and impact of their own testimonies. This reflection encourages us to ask how our personal experiences with the divine shape our faith and our willingness to share that faith with others.

Visions of the Future and Hope

John's revelations provide a comprehensive vision of the future, including the trials and ultimate triumph of God's kingdom. These visions offer not just warnings but also immense hope— promising victory over evil and eternal life for the faithful. Reflecting on John's prophetic revelations inspires us to maintain hope and perseverance, looking forward to the fulfillment of God's promises, no matter the current challenges.

In sum, John the Apostle, as discussed in the Book of Mormon and the Bible, embodies the essence of a true disciple and visionary prophet. His life and writings continue to inspire millions with messages of love, truth, and hope. Reflecting on his contributions not only enriches our understanding of the gospel but also deepens our commitment to live according to the profound truths he championed.

Author's Reflection

As I reflect on the lives of Jesus Christ and John, I am overwhelmed by the depth of their influence, not only in their own time but throughout all of human history. These two figures, one being the Savior of the world and the other His beloved disciple, embody the essence of divine love, truth, and witness. Their lives and teachings offer profound guidance for our own spiritual journeys, especially as we seek to navigate the challenges and opportunities that lead us toward our own promised lands—whether they be spiritual, familial, or communal.

Jesus Christ: The Exemplar of Divine Love and Redemption

Jesus Christ, the central figure of all scripture and the Savior of mankind is the ultimate example of faith, obedience, and love. His life, ministry, and Atonement are the foundation upon which all hope of salvation rests. Christ's teachings, as recorded in the Gospels and the Book of Mormon, emphasize the importance of love (John 13:34-35), faith (Mark 11:22-24), repentance (Luke 13:3), and the necessity of following Him (Matthew 16:24). His atoning sacrifice, which encompasses both His suffering in Gethsemane and His crucifixion, offers the means for all humanity to be redeemed and to inherit eternal life (Alma 7:11-13).

Reflecting on Jesus Christ's life, I am struck by His unwavering commitment to the will of the Father and His boundless compassion for all of God's children. His willingness to suffer and die for the sins of the world is the ultimate expression of love and sacrifice. In our modern lives, Christ's example challenges us to live in a manner that reflects His teachings and His love. His life teaches us that the journey to our promised lands—be they spiritual goals, personal achievements, or communal well-being—must be rooted in faith, humility, and a willingness to serve others.

Christ's teachings on love, particularly the commandment to "love one another as I have loved you" (John 13:34), remind us that our relationships with others are a crucial part of our spiritual journey. In pursuing our promised lands, we must not only seek our own salvation but also help others along the way. Jesus's life exemplifies the idea that true leadership is service, and true power is found in self-sacrifice. His Atonement provides the means for us to overcome sin and death, offering us the ultimate path to our eternal promised land.

John: Apostle of Testimony and Vision

John, often referred to as the "beloved disciple," is a figure whose life and writings provide a powerful witness of Jesus Christ's divinity and mission. John's Gospel focuses on the divine nature of Christ, emphasizing His role as the Light of the World (John 1:4-9), the Good Shepherd (John 10:11-16), and the source of eternal life (John 17:3). Additionally, John's vision recorded in the Book of Revelation provides profound insights into the ultimate triumph of good over evil and the establishment of God's eternal kingdom (Revelation 21:1-4).

Reflecting on John's life, I am inspired by his unwavering testimony of Christ and his deep spiritual insight. John's writings are filled with symbolism and profound theological truths, yet they are also deeply personal, reflecting his close relationship with the Savior. In modern contexts, John's example challenges us to bear witness of Christ in our own lives, to stand firm in our testimony even when faced with opposition or uncertainty. His life teaches us the importance of maintaining a close and personal relationship with the Savior, recognizing that such a relationship is the foundation of all spiritual knowledge and power.

John's vision in Revelation offers a hopeful perspective on the challenges we face in our journey toward our promised lands. It reminds us that despite the trials and tribulations we may encounter, God's purposes will ultimately prevail. The imagery of the New Jerusalem, a symbol of the ultimate promised land, encourages us to look forward with hope and faith, trusting that God's plan for us is one of victory and peace. John's life and writings call us to be witnesses of Christ's love and truth in all that we do, ensuring that *our journey toward the promised land is guided by divine light and eternal vision.*

Summary

Jesus Christ, the Exemplar of Divine Love and Redemption, shows us that our journey must be rooted in love, service, and obedience to God's will, with His Atonement as our pathway to eternal life. John, the Apostle of Testimony and Vision, calls us to bear witness of Christ and hold fast to the hope of God's eternal promises. Together, their teachings guide us toward our promised lands by encouraging us to follow the Savior with unwavering faith and trust in His divine plan.

As I reflect on these figures, I am inspired to cultivate these qualities in my own life. Their teachings challenge us to live with love, to serve others selflessly, and to bear witness to Christ's truth in all that we do. Whether in our personal lives, our families, or our communities, the examples of Jesus Christ and John remind us that our ultimate success in reaching our promised lands depends on our willingness to follow the Savior, to love as He loved, and to trust in the divine plan that guides us toward eternal life.

Chapter 9

The Divine Mother

Essential to Jesus Christ as the redeemer narrative in the Book of Mormon and the prophecies of the Nephite people is the role of Mary, the mother of Jesus Christ. This chapter explores the significance of Mary as portrayed in the Book of Mormon, particularly through the revelations received by Nephi. Understanding her role and the context of her inclusion provides profound insights into the divine plan of salvation and the fulfillment of messianic prophecies.

Historical Context

The prophetic writings and revelations contained in the Book of Mormon place a significant emphasis on the coming of Jesus Christ, the Messiah, and His mortal ministry. Among these prophecies is the foretelling of His birth to a pure and chosen vessel—Mary. The Nephites, having access to the writings of prophets such as Isaiah and other ancient scriptures on the Brass Plates, had a deep-seated expectation of the Messiah's arrival and the circumstances surrounding His birth. The Nephites, influenced by the prophetic writings on the Brass Plates, saw Mary not just as the mother of Jesus, but as a pivotal figure in the fulfillment of ancient prophecies. Her role was deeply intertwined with their understanding of the Messiah's advent, and her life served as a tangible connection to the divine promises they held dear.

Characters in Chapter 9

- **Mary** - The mother of Jesus Christ, exemplified for her purity, divine selection, and crucial role in the fulfillment of messianic prophecies.

This historical context emphasizes Mary's pivotal role within the prophetic framework of the Book of Mormon. As the chosen mother of the Savior, her life exemplifies the fulfillment of ancient prophecies and the divine orchestration of the plan of salvation.

Understanding Mary's significance deepens our appreciation for the sacred narratives and the profound reverence with which the Nephite prophets regarded the birth and mission of Jesus Christ. Nephite leaders likely drew upon Mary's example to teach essential principles of faith, obedience, and divine motherhood, illustrating that even the humblest individuals can play a central role in God's plan. Her life stood as a powerful testament to the Nephites, embodying the strength found in purity and unwavering faith. Inspired by her example, Nephite prophets likely emphasized these virtues in their teachings, using Mary as a model for living a Christ-centered life, and enriching their understanding of the profound spiritual heritage conveyed in the Book of Mormon.

Mary: A Model of Submission and Devotion

Mary, the mother of Jesus, exemplifies profound Christlike virtues such as humility, obedience, and faith. Her life reflects a deep commitment to God's will, evident from her response to the Annunciation when she learns of her role in the birth of the Savior: "Behold the handmaid of the Lord; be it unto me according to thy word" (Luke 1:38). This submission to divine will showcases her humility and acceptance of God's plan without reservation. In the Book of Mormon, Nephi sees Mary in a vision and describes her as a "virgin, most beautiful and fair above all other virgins" (1 Nephi 11:13), emphasizing her purity and righteousness, which are hallmarks of her Christlike character.

Nephi's vision of Mary not only confirmed her role as the mother of the Messiah but also reinforced the Nephite belief in the sacredness of her mission. This vision may have deepened their reverence for the coming of Jesus Christ and the divine orchestration of His birth.

Lessons and Teachings from Mary's Life

Mary's life, as depicted in both the Bible and the Book of Mormon **(1 Nephi 11:13-18)**, provides profound lessons on faith, obedience, and the role of individuals in God's divine plan.

Faith in Divine Purposes

Mary's acceptance of her call to be the mother of the Messiah without fully knowing the implications is a testament to her extraordinary faith. Her situation could have led to severe social stigma; however, her unwavering trust in God's promises reflects a deep-rooted faith that God's plans are right and just. This teaches us about the importance of faith when we face uncertain or challenging circumstances, encouraging us to trust in divine purposes even when we do not fully understand them.

Humility and Service

Throughout her life, Mary exhibits humility and a servile heart. From her initial submission to God's will to her quiet presence at key moments in Jesus' ministry, she demonstrates what it means to serve faithfully and humbly without seeking the spotlight. Her example prompts a reflection on how we embrace roles that might seem lowly or unnoticed, recognizing the value in serving others quietly and faithfully.

Enduring Sorrow with Grace

Mary's journey was not without sorrow. Simeon's prophecy that a sword would pierce her soul (Luke 2:35) is fulfilled in the crucifixion of Jesus, a moment of profound pain and endurance for any mother. Her strength in staying near Jesus during His crucifixion speaks volumes about her courage and love. This aspect of her life offers lessons in handling personal grief and loss with grace, reminding us of the strength found in steadfast love and faith even in the darkest times.

Influence and Legacy

Mary's influence extends beyond her lifetime, affecting countless generations. Her role in the salvation narrative teaches us about the impact one life can have when aligned with God's will. It challenges us to consider the legacy we are creating through our daily choices and acts of faith.

In sum, Mary, as a significant figure both in Christianity and in the Book of Mormon, exemplifies a life of service, humility, and profound faith. Her story encourages us to live with dedication to God's will, enduring grace under pressure, and maintaining a legacy of faith that influences others and fulfills divine purposes. Through her example, we learn the power of simple, steadfast faith and the beauty of a life committed to serving higher, sacred purposes.

Author's Reflection

Reflecting on the life of Mary, the Mother of Jesus, I am deeply moved by her unparalleled example of faith, humility, and unwavering commitment to God's will. As the chosen vessel through whom the Savior of the world would be born, Mary's life is a testament to the power of divine purpose and the extraordinary strength found in humble obedience. Her story, though often told with reverence, holds profound lessons for us today as we seek to fulfill our own divine missions and journey toward our promised lands.

Mary: A Model of Submission and Devotion

Mary's life is marked by her remarkable acceptance of God's will, even in the face of uncertainty and potential social ostracism. When the angel Gabriel appeared to her, announcing that she would conceive and bear the Son of God (Luke 1:26-38), Mary responded with humility and faith, saying, "Behold the handmaid of the Lord; be it unto me according to thy word" (Luke 1:38). This simple yet profound statement encapsulates Mary's entire approach to her life—one of complete submission to God's plan, even when it demanded immense personal sacrifice.

Reflecting on Mary's response to the angel, I am struck by her extraordinary faith and trust in God. She accepted a divine mission that would alter the course of her life and that of humanity, knowing that it would bring both great joy and great sorrow. Mary's example challenges us to consider how we respond to the divine callings in our own lives. Are we, like Mary, willing to say "yes" to God, even when the path ahead is unclear or daunting? Her life teaches us that true faith is not just belief but an active willingness to submit our will to God's, trusting that His plans for us are greater than our own.

In modern contexts, Mary's example is particularly relevant as we navigate the complexities of personal and communal responsibilities. Whether we are called to lead, to serve, or to endure trials, Mary's life reminds us that our journey to the promised land—be it spiritual fulfillment, family unity, or community harmony—requires a heart that is open to God's guidance and a spirit willing to embrace the unknown.

Mary: The Embodiment of Grace and Strength

Mary's life was not without its challenges. From the moment of Jesus's birth, through the flight to Egypt (Matthew 2:13-14), to witnessing her Son's crucifixion (John 19:25-27), Mary demonstrated a quiet strength and grace that is both awe-inspiring and deeply instructive. Despite the hardships and the profound sorrow she endured, particularly as she stood at the foot of the cross, Mary remained steadfast in her faith and her love for her Son.

Reflecting on Mary's life, I am moved by her extraordinary faith and humility. Her willingness to embrace God's plan, despite the uncertainties, teaches us that true faith is not just belief but an active, trusting submission to God's will. Her example challenges us to approach our own divine callings with the same openness and trust, knowing that God's plans are always for our ultimate good.

In modern life, Mary's story resonates with anyone who has faced trials, particularly those that involve deep personal loss or sacrifice. Her example provides comfort and strength, reminding us that we are never alone in our suffering and that God's grace is sufficient to carry us through even the darkest of times.

In our daily lives, we can follow Mary's example by embracing our responsibilities with humility, seeking God's guidance in every decision, and nurturing our relationships with love and patience. These practices will help us align more closely with God's will and navigate the challenges of life with grace.

Mary: A Mother's Love and a Disciple's Faith

Mary's role as the mother of Jesus is often highlighted, but her life also exemplifies the journey of a true disciple. Her presence at key moments in Jesus's life—such as at the wedding in Cana *where she prompted His first miracle (John 2:1-11), and at the cross where Jesus entrusted her care to the beloved disciple John (John 19:26-27)—demonstrates her deep understanding of and commitment to His mission. Mary was not just a mother; she was also a disciple who followed her Son's teachings and supported His ministry.*

Reflecting on Mary's dual role as mother and disciple, I see a powerful example of how our personal relationships can be intertwined with our spiritual missions. Mary's life teaches us that love and faith are not mutually exclusive but are deeply connected. Her nurturing love for Jesus and her unwavering faith in His divine mission challenge us to cultivate both love and faith in our own lives. As we journey toward our promised lands, whether in the context of family, community, or personal spiritual growth, Mary's life reminds us that our relationships with others are a vital part of our spiritual journey. Her example encourages us to nurture those around us with love while remaining steadfast in our faith, knowing that these are the qualities that will help us fulfill our divine purposes.

Summary

Mary, the Mother of Jesus, embodies profound lessons in faith, humility, grace, and love. Her life serves as a timeless guide for our personal spiritual growth and the well-being of our communities as we strive toward our own promised lands.

Mary's steadfast submission to God's will encourages us to approach our divine callings with faith and trust, even when the future is uncertain. Her grace and strength in the face of significant challenges illustrate that true faith involves enduring trials with love and unwavering confidence in God's plan. Her dual role as both mother and disciple highlights the deep connection between our personal relationships and spiritual missions, reminding us that nurturing both is vital to fulfilling our divine purposes.

Mary's life stands as a testament to the transformative power of faith, humility, and love in realizing God's purposes. Her example inspires us to embrace our divine callings with trust and to nurture those around us with grace and compassion. Reflecting on her journey, we see that success in reaching our promised lands depends on our willingness to follow God's plan, love deeply, and rely on His grace to guide us through life's challenges.

Part V

Culmination of the Nephite

Chronicles

Part V concludes the epic narrative from the Small Plates of Nephi, chronicling the journey of the Nephite people from their departure from Jerusalem to their arrival in Zarahemla. This section explores the critical contributions of the final prophet-historians and the restoration of their sacred records in the latter days. Comprising two chapters, Part V examines the culmination of the Nephite chronicles, highlighting the preservation of the Nephite legacy and its ultimate fulfillment through the restoration of the gospel.

These chapters emphasize the preservation of sacred records and the fulfillment of prophetic purposes in the latter days. They underscore the pivotal roles of Mormon and Moroni in documenting and safeguarding Nephite history, as well as the divine orchestration that brought these records to light through Joseph Smith. This culmination not only secures the Nephite legacy but also reinforces the enduring relevance of their teachings in the restored gospel of Jesus Christ.

The Small Plates of Nephi: An Explanation

The Small Plates of Nephi were a set of records created by Nephi, the son of Lehi, as he was commanded by God to do so. Unlike the larger plates, which focused on the historical and political events of the Nephite people, the Small Plates were primarily concerned with spiritual matters, including prophecies, teachings, and the dealings of God with His people. These plates were a spiritual record meant to preserve the teachings and testimonies of the early Nephite prophets and to serve as a witness of Jesus Christ.

Mormon, one of the last Nephite prophet-historians, discovered the Small Plates and, recognizing their spiritual significance, decided to include them in his abridgment of the Nephite record. He incorporated them without alteration, seeing them as an inspired addition that could complement his own abridged account. Mormon was guided by the Spirit to preserve these records for future generations, even though he did not fully understand the reason at the time. His son Moroni, the last Nephite prophet, continued this effort by safeguarding these records until they were eventually delivered to Joseph Smith in the 19th century.

The inclusion of the Small Plates of Nephi in the Book of Mormon was not only a fulfillment of divine instruction but also a means to ensure that vital spiritual teachings and prophecies would be preserved and available to future generations. These records were crucial in the restoration of the gospel, providing a second witness of Jesus Christ and playing a key role in the unfolding of God's plan in the latter days.

Culmination of the Nephite Chronicles

Together, the chapters in Part V illustrate the culmination of the Nephite chronicles through the preservation of their sacred records and the fulfillment of their prophetic purpose in the latter days. They emphasize the critical roles of Mormon and Moroni in documenting and safeguarding Nephite history, and the divine orchestration that brought these records to light through Joseph Smith. This culmination not only preserves the Nephite legacy but also reinforces the enduring relevance of their teachings in the restored gospel of Jesus Christ.

Chapter 10

Final Prophet-Historians

The concluding chapters of the Nephite record are shaped by the devoted efforts of two final prophet-historians: Mormon and his son, Moroni. These figures played a crucial role in compiling, preserving, and safeguarding the sacred records of their people. Their lives and contributions provide invaluable insights into the challenges faced by the Nephite civilization in its final days and underscore the enduring importance of faith, resilience, and divine guidance.

Historical Context

The era in which Mormon and Moroni lived was one of immense turmoil and decline for the Nephite civilization. By the fourth and fifth centuries AD, the Nephites were locked in relentless warfare with the Lamanites, leading to widespread destruction and the eventual annihilation of the Nephite nation. Amidst this chaos, Mormon and Moroni were entrusted with the sacred responsibility of compiling and preserving the records that documented their history, teachings, and prophecies.

Characters in Chapter 10

- **Mormon** ~ The prophet-historian who abridged the Nephite records, led the Nephite armies, and preserved the teachings for future generations.
- **Moroni** ~ The last Nephite prophet, who completed his father's work, abridged the Book of Ether, and safeguarded the records for future revelation.

This historical context provides a backdrop for understanding the immense challenges faced by Mormon and Moroni as they fulfilled their divine responsibilities. Their efforts to compile and protect the sacred records amidst the collapse of their civilization highlight themes of resilience, faith, and the importance of preserving spiritual truths for future generations. Through their writings, Mormon and Moroni offer timeless lessons on enduring faith, the consequences of societal decay, and the hope of redemption through Jesus Christ. Their legacy, encapsulated in the Book of Mormon, continues to inspire and guide believers around the world.

Mormon: A Steward of Sacred Records

Mormon, a central figure in the compilation of the Book of Mormon **(Words of Mormon 3-8)**, exhibits profound Christlike attributes such as wisdom, foresight, and obedience. As a historian and a prophet, his decision to include the small plates of Nephi with his other records is a testament to his spiritual discernment and dedication to God's directives. Mormon's careful stewardship of these sacred texts underscores his commitment to truth and his deep reverence for God's word. His actions reveal a leader who is both thoughtful and inspired, ensuring the preservation of essential teachings for future generations.

Lessons and Teachings from Mormon's Inclusion of the Small Plates

The Importance of Obedience to Divine Promptings

Mormon's decision to include the small plates of Nephi, as he reports, comes after feeling inspired by the Spirit (Words of Mormon 1:7). This act of obedience to spiritual promptings underscores the importance of being attuned to divine guidance in our decision-making processes. It teaches us that even in duties that seem clear-cut, being open to further revelation can lead to actions of significant long-term importance. Reflecting on this, we might consider how we respond to divine promptings. Do we listen and act upon them with the same trust and obedience that Mormon showed?

Stewardship of Sacred Knowledge

By adding the small plates to his compilation, Mormon demonstrates exemplary stewardship of sacred knowledge. He recognizes the intrinsic value of these records, not for their historical detail alone but for their great worth of the teachings they contain. This action teaches us about the critical responsibility we have in preserving and valuing the knowledge and wisdom passed down to us. Are we careful stewards of the knowledge and traditions entrusted to us? How do we ensure that these are preserved and appreciated appropriately?

Foresight and the Legacy for Future Generations

Mormon's inclusion of the small plates is a decision made with an eye towards future generations, a hallmark of true foresight. He understands that these records will benefit others far beyond his time. This perspective invites us to think about the impact of our actions on future generations. Do we consider the long-term effects of our decisions? Are we working to leave a legacy that will guide and benefit those who follow us?

Commitment to Truth and Completeness

Mormon's careful compilation of the records, ensuring that nothing of value was lost, highlights his commitment to truth and the completeness of the scriptural message. This teaches us the importance of thoroughness and integrity in our work, especially when it involves principles or teachings that can guide others. Reflecting on this, we might consider how we handle responsibilities involving the dissemination of information or teachings. Do we strive for accuracy and completeness?

In sum, Mormon's actions regarding the small plates teach us about obedience, stewardship, foresight, and integrity. These lessons are not only vital for personal development but are also essential in any leadership or custodial role we might hold. His example encourages us to be diligent and inspired stewards of the resources and knowledge we possess, ensuring their benefit and preservation for the future.

Moroni: Diligence, Faith, and Integrity in Stewardship

Moroni, the final prophet-historian of the Nephites **(Introduction to the Book of Mormon)**, exhibited profound Christlike attributes, including diligence, faith, and integrity. As the custodian of his people's records, Moroni's actions in compiling, hiding, and eventually delivering these sacred texts to Joseph Smith reflect his unwavering commitment to God's commands and his deep concern for future generations. His meticulous care in preserving the records, despite the imminent destruction of his people, showcases his dedication and foresight. Moreover, his appearance as a resurrected being to Joseph Smith, entrusting him with these sacred writings, underscores his role as a faithful messenger and guardian of divine knowledge.

Lessons and Teachings from Moroni's Life and Actions

Stewardship and Diligence

Moroni's meticulous effort in compiling and preserving the records of his people demonstrates exceptional stewardship and diligence. This reflects a Christlike dedication to fulfilling God's commands meticulously and responsibly. Moroni's actions remind us of the importance of being diligent stewards of what we are entrusted with, whether these are material possessions, spiritual gifts, or knowledge. We learn that true diligence involves not just the preservation of physical items but also the safeguarding of knowledge and heritage for future benefit.

Faith Amid Desolation

Operating in a time of great despair and isolation, Moroni's unwavering faith is particularly striking. His ability to focus on a mission for a future he would not see in his lifetime shows immense spiritual strength and conviction. This teaches us about the nature of prophetic faith—seeing beyond current circumstances and working towards a divine promise. Reflecting on this, we might ask ourselves how we act on our faith. Are we prepared to work tirelessly towards goals we may never see fulfilled in our lifetime but believe are critical for future generations?

Integrity in Isolation

The integrity of Moroni, acting alone after the destruction of his people, highlights his moral fortitude. Without the support of a community or immediate feedback on his actions, Moroni remained true to his principles and commitments. This integrity in isolation teaches us that true character is demonstrated not in public accolades but in our private decisions and actions. It challenges us to maintain our values consistently, regardless of our circumstances or the presence of others.

Messenger of Restoration

Finally, Moroni's role in delivering the plates to Joseph Smith illustrates the continuity of God's work across dispensations. He bridges the ancient and modern, acting as a messenger who initiates the restoration of the gospel. This teaches us about the eternal nature of God's plan and the interconnectedness of all dispensations in His work. Reflecting on this, we see the importance of each individual's role in God's broader plan, inspiring us to seek out and fulfill our part in divine purposes.

In sum, Moroni's life and his pivotal actions in preserving and delivering the Nephite records offer profound lessons in stewardship, faith, integrity, and the eternal nature of God's work. His example encourages us to apply these principles in our lives, ensuring that we act diligently, maintain faith through trials, uphold integrity at all times, and contribute faithfully to God's ongoing work on Earth.

Author's Reflection

As I reflect on the lives of Mormon and Moroni, I am deeply moved by their unwavering commitment to preserving the spiritual legacy of their people amidst the collapse of their civilization. These two prophets, father and son, stand as monumental figures of faith, resilience, and duty in the face of overwhelming adversity. Their lives and teachings offer profound insights into the importance of stewardship, perseverance, and hope, especially when the promised lands we seek seem distant or unattainable. Their example challenges us to remain steadfast in our faith and responsibilities, even when all around us appears to be falling apart.

Mormon: A Steward of Sacred Records and Faith

Mormon's life is marked by his incredible dedication to the preservation of the Nephite records, a task he took on at the young age of ten (Mormon 1:2). As a military leader, historian, and prophet, Mormon faced the tragic decline of his people, yet he remained faithful to his duty to compile and abridge the sacred records that would become the Book of Mormon (Mormon 2:17-19). His writings reveal a man deeply committed to the truth and to the future of the gospel, even when his present circumstances were filled with sorrow and despair.

Reflecting on Mormon's life, I see a powerful example of stewardship and faith in the face of overwhelming odds. Mormon's determination to preserve the Nephite records, despite witnessing the complete moral decay of his people (Mormon 5:2), teaches us about the importance of maintaining our responsibilities, even when it seems that our efforts may be in vain. In our modern lives, Mormon's example challenges us to think about how we handle our own sacred trusts—whether they be spiritual, familial, or communal. Are we, like Mormon, willing to persevere in our duties, knowing that our work may bless future generations even if we do not see the results in our lifetime?

Mormon's ability to remain faithful to God despite the widespread wickedness around him also speaks to the importance of maintaining personal integrity and commitment to divine principles, regardless of external circumstances. His life reminds us that our journey to the promised land is not just about reaching a destination but about how we conduct ourselves along the way. Mormon's steadfastness in compiling the sacred records and his efforts to call his people to repentance (Mormon 3:2-3) teach us that faithfulness to God's commandments and a commitment to truth are essential, even in the darkest of times.

Moroni: Diligence, Faith, and Integrity in Stewardship

Moroni, the son of Mormon, is the final prophet in the Book of Mormon, and his life is one of profound loneliness, endurance, and hope. After witnessing the destruction of his people, Moroni took up the mantle of his father's work, adding his own writings and finalizing the record that would be hidden for future generations (Moroni 10:1-2). Moroni's writings, including his reflections on faith, hope, and charity (Moroni 7:40-48), his exhortations to future readers (Mormon 9:27-31), and his account of the ordinances and structure of the Church (Moroni 2-6), reveal a deep concern for the spiritual welfare of those who would eventually receive the records.

Reflecting on Moroni's life, I am struck by his incredible perseverance and faith despite the complete destruction of his people. Living alone and constantly on the run (Moroni 1:1-3), Moroni continued to fulfill his divine responsibilities, knowing that his efforts were crucial for future generations. His life teaches us the importance of diligence and faith, even when it seems that all hope is lost. In modern contexts, Moroni's example challenges us to remain faithful to our commitments and to trust that God's purposes will be fulfilled, even if we do not see the immediate results of our labors.

Moroni's reflections on faith, hope, and charity in Moroni 7 offer profound insights into the attributes that are essential for personal and communal spiritual growth. His teachings remind us that faith in Jesus Christ, hope in His promises, and the pure love of Christ (charity) are the foundations upon which our journey to the promised land must be built. Moroni's life exemplifies these principles, as he remained hopeful and full of love even as he witnessed the complete destruction of his civilization.

Summary

The characters of Chapter 10—Mormon and Moroni—offer profound lessons in faith, stewardship, and perseverance. Their lives, filled with challenges and profound responsibilities, provide timeless guidance for us as we navigate our own journeys toward the promised land, especially in times of difficulty and uncertainty.

Mormon's life teaches us the importance of being diligent stewards of the spiritual, familial, and communal responsibilities we have been given. His example challenges us to remain faithful to our duties, even when it seems that our efforts may be in vain, trusting that our work will have a lasting impact on future generations.

Moroni's life exemplifies the principles of faith, hope, and charity. His perseverance in completing the sacred records, despite living in isolation and constant danger, teaches us about the importance of remaining steadfast in our commitments and trusting in God's purposes, even when we cannot see the immediate results of our efforts.

As I reflect on the lives of Mormon and Moroni, I am inspired to cultivate these qualities in my own life. Their teachings challenge us to live with integrity, to be diligent in our stewardship, and to maintain faith and hope, even in the most challenging circumstances. Whether in our personal lives, our families, or our communities, the examples of Mormon and Moroni remind us that our ultimate success in reaching our promised lands depends on our willingness to remain faithful to God's commandments, to persevere in our duties, and to trust in His divine purposes, knowing that our efforts will ultimately contribute to the fulfillment of His eternal plan.

Chapter 11

Restoration in the Latter Days

The culmination of the Nephite record is intricately tied to the divine restoration of the gospel in the latter days. This chapter focuses on the pivotal figures involved in this miraculous event: Moroni, the last Nephite prophet, and Joseph Smith, the prophet of the Restoration. Understanding their roles provides a profound perspective on the fulfillment of ancient prophecies and the unfolding of God's plan to restore His church in the latter days.

Historical Context

The Book of Mormon records were hidden by **Moroni** around AD 421, with the promise that they would come forth in a future time when God would once again establish His truth among men. This promise was fulfilled in the early 19th century, a period marked by religious revival and fervent searching for truth in the United States. The spiritual environment of this era set the stage for the remarkable events that would lead to the restoration of the gospel.

Characters in Chapter 11

- **Moroni -** The last Nephite prophet who preserved and hid the records, and later appeared as a resurrected being to Joseph Smith, guiding him to the plates. (See Chapter 10)
- **Joseph Smith -** The prophet of the Restoration, who translated the Book of Mormon and re-established the Church of Jesus Christ in the latter days.

This historical context emphasizes the extraordinary roles of **Moroni** and **Joseph Smith** in the restoration of the gospel. **Moroni**'s diligent preservation of the records and his divine mission to deliver them to **Joseph Smith** underscore the continuity and fulfillment of God's promises. **Joseph Smith**'s visionary experiences and his translation of the Book of Mormon represent the fulfillment of ancient prophecies and the re-establishment of God's church on earth. Together, their contributions highlight themes of divine guidance, prophetic fulfillment, and the enduring power of faith. The restoration of the gospel through their efforts continues to impact millions of lives, reaffirming the eternal truths of the Book of Mormon and the reality of God's ongoing work among His children.

Joseph Smith: A Conduit of Revelation and Restoration

Joseph Smith, the founder of the Church of Jesus Christ of Latter-day Saints (JS History 1), demonstrated numerous Christlike attributes through his role in translating the Book of Mormon. His unwavering faith, perseverance against adversity, humility in seeking divine guidance, and dedication to his prophetic mission mirror the virtues that Christ exemplified throughout His ministry. As a young man faced with profound spiritual responsibilities, **Joseph Smith**'s trust in God and his commitment to translating the sacred plates exemplify a steadfast devotion to doing the Lord's work despite formidable challenges.

Lessons and Teachings from Joseph Smith's Translation of the Book of Mormon

Faith and Revelation

Joseph Smith's experience with translating the Book of Mormon underscores the importance of faith in the pursuit of divine revelation. As he worked on the translation, **Joseph** relied not on scholarly tools or prior scriptural knowledge but on the power of God through the means of the Urim and Thummim and later, direct inspiration. This reliance teaches us about the nature of true faith—grounded not in seeing but in believing and trusting that God will provide the means for His work to be accomplished (1 Nephi 3:7). Reflecting on this, we can assess how we approach challenges that require faith. Do we move forward with trust in divine assistance, even when the path is not clear?

Perseverance Through Adversity

Throughout the translation process, **Joseph** faced significant opposition, both from individuals close to him and from broader societal forces. His determination to continue despite these obstacles illustrates a profound lesson in perseverance and resilience. The scriptures in the Book of Mormon itself reinforce this lesson, as prophets like Nephi and Moroni also faced severe trials but remained steadfast in their missions (1 Nephi 7:17). **Joseph**'s perseverance invites us to consider how we handle opposition or hardship. Are we committed to our goals with the same tenacity?

Humility and Learning

Joseph's approach to translating the Book of Mormon also highlights his humility. He readily acknowledged his dependence on divine guidance and admitted his own weaknesses (Joseph Smith—History 1:29). This humility allowed him to be an effective instrument in God's hands, a key trait for anyone wishing to serve or lead others effectively. Reflecting on this, we might ask how humility plays a role in our endeavors. Do we acknowledge our limitations and seek divine help?

Legacy of Diligence and Integrity

The legacy of **Joseph Smith** in translating the Book of Mormon teaches us about the impact of diligence and integrity in fulfilling one's duties. His meticulous care in translating and protecting the plates, ensuring their message was conveyed accurately and respectfully, sets a standard for how we should treat responsibilities that have lasting implications. Reflecting on this, we can evaluate our commitment to the tasks we are given. Are we as diligent and conscientious in ensuring our work is done to the best of our abilities and with integrity?

In sum, **Joseph Smith**'s role in translating the Book of Mormon offers enduring lessons in faith, perseverance, humility, and diligence. His life and work challenge us to apply these principles in our personal and spiritual journeys, encouraging us to seek divine guidance, overcome adversities with resilience, approach our tasks with humility, and perform our duties with unwavering integrity and diligence.

Author's Reflection

*As I reflect on the life and mission of **Joseph Smith**, the Prophet of the Restoration, I am struck by the profound impact his life and teachings have had on the course of religious history. **Joseph Smith**'s role in restoring the gospel of Jesus Christ, translating the Book of Mormon, and establishing the Church of Jesus Christ of Latter-day Saints is a testament to the power of faith, revelation, and divine guidance. His experiences and teachings offer invaluable lessons for our own spiritual journeys, especially as we strive to reach our promised lands—whether they be personal, familial, or communal.*

Joseph Smith: A Prophet of Revelation and Restoration

* **Joseph Smith**'s life is marked by his unwavering faith in divine revelation and his role as a chosen instrument in God's hands to restore the fullness of the gospel. From his First Vision at the age of fourteen, where he saw God the Father and Jesus Christ (Joseph Smith—History 1:17-20), to the translation of the Book of Mormon through the gift and power of God (Doctrine and Covenants 135:3), **Joseph**'s life was characterized by a constant flow of divine instruction and guidance. His dedication to his prophetic mission,*

despite relentless persecution, stands as a powerful example of faith and perseverance.

*Reflecting on **Joseph Smith**'s life, I am deeply inspired by his courage and commitment to follow God's direction, even when it led to great personal sacrifice. **Joseph**'s example challenges us to consider how we respond to divine promptings in our own lives. Are we, like **Joseph**, willing to trust in God's plan, even when it requires us to step into the unknown or face significant opposition? His life teaches us that the journey to our promised lands often involves trials that test our faith, but with trust in God's guidance, we can accomplish the purposes He has for us.*

***Joseph**'s experiences with revelation, particularly the translation of the Book of Mormon, also highlight the importance of seeking and receiving divine guidance in our lives. His life encourages us to cultivate a personal relationship with God, to seek His will through prayer, and to be open to the promptings of the Holy Spirit. As we navigate our own spiritual journeys, **Joseph**'s example reminds us that divine revelation is not just a historical event but an ongoing process that can guide us toward our own promised lands.*

The Restoration: A Divine Plan for the Last Days

The Restoration of the gospel through **Joseph Smith** *was not merely a historical event but the fulfillment of ancient prophecies and the initiation of a new era in God's plan for His children. The coming forth of the Book of Mormon, the establishment of the Church, and the restoration of priesthood authority are all part of the unfolding of God's work in the last days (Doctrine and Covenants 27:13).* **Joseph**'s *role in this divine plan underscores the importance of each of us recognizing and fulfilling our roles in God's work.*

Reflecting on the Restoration, I see a powerful message about the importance of being instruments in God's hands. Just as **Joseph Smith** *was called to restore the gospel, we too are called to participate in God's work, whether through missionary service, temple work, or simply living as examples of Christ's teachings in our daily lives. The Restoration teaches us that each of us has a role to play in the unfolding of God's plan and that by fulfilling our responsibilities, we contribute to the building of His kingdom on earth.*

In modern life, the Restoration also reminds us that God's work is ongoing and that we are part of a larger divine narrative. As we journey toward our own promised lands, whether they be spiritual goals, personal achievements, or communal progress, the

Restoration challenges us to remain faithful to our covenants, to seek God's guidance in all things, and to trust that our efforts are part of His greater plan for humanity.

Joseph Smith's Legacy: A Call to Faith and Perseverance

__Joseph Smith__'s legacy is one of faith, courage, and unwavering dedication to God's work. His teachings, as recorded in the Doctrine and Covenants, continue to guide and inspire millions of people around the world. __Joseph__'s emphasis on the importance of faith, repentance, baptism, and the gift of the Holy Ghost (Doctrine and Covenants 20:37) remains central to the spiritual lives of Latter-day Saints. His life also teaches us about the importance of perseverance in the face of trials and the need to remain true to our convictions, even when faced with overwhelming challenges.

Reflecting on __Joseph__'s legacy, I am reminded of the importance of perseverance in our own spiritual journeys. __Joseph__'s life was filled with trials, including imprisonment, persecution, and ultimately martyrdom (Doctrine and Covenants 135:1-7), yet he remained steadfast in his faith and his commitment to God's work. His example challenges us to remain faithful to our own spiritual commitments, even when we face difficulties or opposition. As we *strive to reach our promised lands, **Joseph**'s life reminds us that perseverance, guided by faith and revelation, is key to overcoming the challenges we encounter along the way.*

Summary

The character of **Joseph Smith** and the events of the Restoration offer profound insights into the principles of faith, revelation, perseverance, and divine purpose. His life and mission provide timeless lessons that are essential for our personal spiritual growth and for the well-being of our communities as we seek to achieve our own promised lands.

Joseph Smith's unwavering faith in divine revelation challenges us to trust in God's guidance, even when it leads us into unknown or difficult circumstances. His role in the Restoration teaches us about the importance of recognizing and fulfilling our roles in God's work and that each of us is part of a larger divine narrative.

As I reflect on **Joseph**'s life and the Restoration, I am inspired to cultivate these qualities in my own journey. His teachings challenge us to live with faith, to seek divine guidance, and to persevere in our spiritual commitments, knowing that our efforts are part of God's greater plan. Whether in our personal lives, our families, or our communities, the example of **Joseph Smith** and the Restoration reminds us that our ultimate success in reaching our promised lands depends on our willingness to follow God's direction, trust in His purposes, and to remain steadfast in our faith, no matter the challenges we face.

Conclusion

As we reach the end of our journey *From Jerusalem to Zarahemla*, we reflect on the powerful foundations of faith that have guided these early Nephite pioneers to their promised land. From Lehi's prophetic leadership and Nephi's unwavering obedience to Mary's humility and Joseph Smith's role in the Restoration, each story we have explored reveals the indispensable role of faith in navigating the challenges of life and achieving divine purposes. These lessons resonate not only in the past but also in our present, guiding us as we seek our own promised lands, whether they be spiritual, familial, or communal.

Yet, the story of the Nephite civilization does not end in Zarahemla. The spiritual journey continues as the Nephites face new challenges, new leaders emerge, and the saga of faith, endurance, and revelation unfolds. From the establishment of Zarahemla as a spiritual and temporal stronghold to the eventual decline of the Nephite nation and the climactic battles at Cumorah, the narrative transitions from building foundations to confronting the inevitable trials of a people striving to maintain their covenant with God.

As we turn the page to *From Zarahemla to Cumorah*, we prepare to explore the next phase of the Nephite story—a phase marked by both the heights of righteousness under inspired leaders and the depths of apostasy and destruction. This journey will take us through the rise and fall of civilizations, the enduring power of faith amidst adversity, and the ultimate fulfillment of divine prophecies. It is a story that underscores the cyclical nature of spiritual growth and decline and reminds us that the journey to the promised land is ongoing, demanding continual faith, repentance, and reliance on divine guidance.

Let us carry forward the lessons learned from *Jerusalem to Zarahemla* as we venture into this next book, where the legacy of the Nephites will be tested like never before. The principles of faith, leadership, and obedience that sustained them in their early years will be both their strength and their challenge as they face the complexities of maintaining a covenant society in an ever-changing world. As we journey *From Zarahemla to Cumorah*, we will see how these enduring principles continue to shape the destiny of the Nephite people—and how they apply to our lives today as we navigate the complexities of our own spiritual journeys.

Author's Reflection

Reflecting on the characters across **From Jerusalem to Zarahemla**, I am struck by the profound depth of their faith, the diversity of their experiences, and the timeless lessons they offer for our own journeys toward our promised lands. Each character, from ancient prophets to latter-day seers, exemplifies unique virtues and challenges that are as relevant today as they were in their own times. Through their lives, we learn about the nature of divine guidance, the power of faith and obedience, the importance of perseverance, and the necessity of love and service. These insights are invaluable as we navigate the complexities of modern life, striving to fulfill our divine purposes individually and collectively.

Chapter 1 ~ The Prophetic Family

- *Lehi's life exemplifies the importance of spiritual foresight and obedience to divine direction. His immediate response to leave Jerusalem upon receiving revelation (1 Nephi 2:2) teaches us that our journey to promised lands often requires leaving behind familiar comforts for uncertain futures. Lehi's unwavering faith in God's promises challenges us to trust in divine guidance, especially when it leads us into the unknown.*

- *Sariah's* journey from doubt to firm testimony (1 Nephi 5:8) is a powerful reminder that faith often deepens through trials. Her experience teaches us that moments of uncertainty are natural, but through perseverance, our faith can become a source of strength for ourselves and our families.

- *Nephi's* declaration, "I will go and do" (1 Nephi 3:7), illustrates the principle of proactive faith. His life reminds us that faith in God must be accompanied by action. Nephi's leadership teaches us that achieving our promised lands requires both trust in God and the willingness to take bold, decisive steps forward.

- *Sam's* quiet loyalty (1 Nephi 2:17) teaches us the value of steadfast support. His life reminds us that every role is crucial in achieving collective goals, and that faithfulness in seemingly small things contributes to the greater good.

- *Jacob's* teachings on justice and the Atonement (2 Nephi 9) highlight the importance of moral integrity and empathy. His life challenges us to apply Christ's teachings in our lives, advocating for justice and relying on divine grace for redemption.

- *Joseph's* connection to ancient prophecies (2 Nephi 3) emphasizes the continuity of God's promises. His life encourages us to see ourselves as part of a larger divine *narrative, reminding us to remain faithful to the promises God has made to us.*

Chapter 2 ~ Reluctant Followers and Adversaries

- **Laban's** *misuse of power (1 Nephi 4:22) serves as a stark warning about the dangers of prioritizing material wealth over spiritual truths. His life teaches us that power must be wielded with integrity, and that failing to do so leads to spiritual and temporal ruin.*

- **Laman's** *struggle with faith and doubt (1 Nephi 2:11-12) highlights the importance of trust in divine guidance. His life reminds us that unresolved doubts can lead to rebellion and division, urging us to confront our uncertainties with faith.*

- **Lemuel's** *susceptibility to influence (1 Nephi 2:13) underscores the importance of developing personal conviction. His life teaches us that without a strong foundation of faith, we are vulnerable to being led astray by external pressures.*

- **Sherem's** *intellectual pride and eventual repentance (Jacob 7:17-19) illustrate the dangers of relying solely on human logic while rejecting spiritual truths. His life challenges us to maintain humility and openness to divine revelation, reminding us that faith often transcends human understanding.*

Chapter 3 ~ Allies from Jerusalem

- ***Zoram's*** *loyalty (1 Nephi 4:31-35) and willingness to join Lehi's family highlight the transformative power of embracing truth and aligning oneself with divine purposes. His life encourages us to leave behind our former ways and fully commit to God's path.*

- ***Ishmael's*** *decision to join Lehi (1 Nephi 7:4-5) emphasizes the importance of unity and collective endurance. His life teaches us that achieving communal goals requires sacrifice and a commitment to the greater good.*

- ***Ishmael's Wife*** *exemplifies quiet strength and unwavering faith during the journey to the promised land. Her life reminds us that often, the most profound acts of faith are those performed without recognition, sustaining families and communities through difficult times.*

- ***Daughter of Ishmael's*** *loyalty (1 Nephi 16:7) and integration into Lehi's family underscores the importance of commitment to collective goals. Her life teaches us that faith and dedication are essential for maintaining unity within families and communities.*

Chapter 4 ~ Secular and Spiritual Leaders

- **Second King of the Nephites'** commitment to preserving Nephi's righteous legacy (Jacob 1:9-10) teaches us the importance of continuity in leadership and the preservation of spiritual foundations.

- **Mosiah's** visionary leadership (Omni 1:12-14) and unification of diverse peoples challenge us to be inclusive and to guide our communities with foresight and faith.

- **Leader of Zarahemla's** humility in joining forces with Mosiah (Omni 1:19) teaches us the value of collaboration and the wisdom of prioritizing communal well-being over personal power.

- **King Benjamin's** teachings on service and humility (Mosiah 2:17) challenge us to lead by example, serving others with love and placing their needs above our own.

Chapter 5 ~ The Record Keepers

- **Enos's** persistent prayer (Enos 1:4) and intercession for his people teach us the power of sincere and enduring faith, reminding us that our spiritual responsibilities extend beyond ourselves.

- ***Jarom's*** *emphasis on stewardship and spiritual vigilance (Jarom 1:10-12) teaches us the importance of preserving and passing on spiritual truths to future generations.*
- ***Omni's*** *acknowledgment of his shortcomings (Omni 1:2-3) yet commitment to continuing the record-keeping tradition reminds us that our contributions, however small, are vital to the greater good.*
- ***Amaron, Chemish, Abinadom, and Amaleki:*** *These record keepers, though brief in their accounts, highlight the importance of each generation's contribution to the preservation of spiritual knowledge, teaching us that every effort to maintain our spiritual heritage is significant.*

Chapter 6 ~ Prophets and Kings of the Brass Plates

- ***Zenock's*** *teachings on the Atonement (1 Nephi 19:10-13) and his willingness to suffer for truth remind us that faith often requires sacrifice and that the Atonement is central to our spiritual journey.*
- ***Neum's*** *prophecy of Christ's crucifixion (1 Nephi 19:10) underscores the importance of bearing witness to fundamental gospel truths, even when they challenge prevailing beliefs.*
- ***Zenos's*** *allegory of the olive tree (Jacob 5) teaches us about God's ongoing efforts to nurture and redeem His people,*

encouraging us to trust in His divine purposes and be patient in our spiritual growth.

- **Zedekiah's** *failures as a leader (Helaman 8:21) serve as a cautionary tale about the consequences of ignoring divine counsel, reminding us that leadership requires humility and adherence to God's will.*

Chapter 7 ~ Major Prophets and Their Teachings

- **Isaiah's** *prophecies (2 Nephi 16; Isaiah 53) emphasize the redemptive power of the Messiah and challenge us to maintain faith in God's promises, even in times of difficulty.*
- **Jeremiah's** *courage in the face of persecution (Jeremiah 20:2) teaches us the importance of standing up for truth and justice, even when it comes at great personal cost.*
- **Moses's** *leadership during the Exodus (Exodus 12:37-42) and his humility (Numbers 12:3) remind us that true leadership is rooted in service and trust in God's guidance.*
- **Joseph's** *forgiveness of his brothers (Genesis 50:20) teaches us about the power of forgiveness and the importance of trusting in God's providence, even in the face of betrayal and hardship.*

Chapter 8 ~ Jesus Christ and His Witnesses

- **Jesus Christ's** life and Atonement (John 13:34-35; 2 Nephi 25:13) are the ultimate examples of love, sacrifice, and obedience. His teachings challenge us to live lives rooted in love and service, guiding others toward their own promised lands.

- **John's** testimony of Christ's divinity (1 Nephi 14:19-27; John 1:4-9) and his vision in Revelation (Revelation 21:1-4) remind us of the importance of bearing witness to the truth and maintaining hope in God's ultimate plan for humanity.

Chapter 9 ~ The Divine Mother

- **Mary's** submission to God's will (1 Nephi 11:15-18; Luke 1:38) and her role as the mother of Jesus Christ teach us about the power of humility, faith, and the quiet strength required to fulfill our divine purposes. Her life challenges us to embrace our roles with grace and trust in God's plan.

Chapter 10 ~ Final Prophet-Historians

- **Mormon's** commitment to preserving the Nephite records (Mormon 1:3-7; 5:2) despite overwhelming adversity teaches us about the importance of stewardship and the need to remain faithful to our responsibilities, even when the outcome seems uncertain.

- ***Moroni's*** *perseverance in finalizing the Book of Mormon (Moroni 10:1-2) and his teachings on faith, hope, and charity (Moroni 7:40-48) remind us that these virtues are essential for personal and communal spiritual growth, especially in times of trial.*

Chapter 11 ~ Restoration in the Latter Days

- ***Joseph Smith's*** *role in the Restoration (Joseph Smith— History 1:17-20) is foreshadowed by the writings of Nephi, which challenge us to seek God's guidance in all things and to trust in His purposes, even when we face significant challenges. His life teaches us that each of us has a role to play in God's work and that by fulfilling our responsibilities, we contribute to the building of His kingdom on earth.*

In sum, as I reflect on the lives and teachings of the characters in **From Jerusalem to Zarahemla**, I am deeply inspired by their unwavering faith, their resilience in the face of trials, and their commitment to divine purposes. Each character offers unique insights that are as relevant today as they were in ancient times. Their lives challenge us to remain faithful, to seek divine guidance, to serve others with love, and to persevere in our spiritual journeys, knowing that our efforts are part of a greater divine plan. Whether in our personal lives, our families, or our communities, the examples of these characters remind us that our ultimate success in reaching our promised lands depends on our willingness to follow God's direction, to trust in His promises, and to live lives rooted in faith, hope, and charity.

Appendices

The Small Plates of Nephi, along with the Brass Plates, within the Book of Mormon encompass a rich tapestry of themes and motifs that are essential to understanding the spiritual and historical trajectory of the Nephite and Lamanite peoples. These themes are presented by way of example only. To receive the full benefit of understanding that comes through the Holy Ghost it is highly recommended to read directly from the Book of Mormon regularly. Here are some key themes derived from the main characters described in these texts:

1. Faith and Obedience

- **Characters**: Nephi, Lehi, and Enos
- **Theme**: Demonstrations of faith and obedience serve as foundational experiences for these characters. Nephi's obedience to God's commands to obtain the brass plates and build a ship (1 Nephi 3:7; 1 Nephi 17:8-9) and Lehi's departure from Jerusalem (1 Nephi 2:2) illustrate how faith leads to divine guidance and protection.

- **Scriptural Reference**: 1 Nephi 3:7 – Nephi expresses his willingness to obey God's commands, emphasizing the theme of unquestioning obedience and its blessings.

2. Prophetic Visions and Revelation

- **Characters**: Nephi, Jacob, and Isaiah (from the Brass Plates)
- **Theme**: Visions and revelations are central to understanding God's will and the destiny of the people. Nephi's vision of the Tree of Life (1 Nephi 8) and his interpretation of his father's dream significantly shapes the theological foundation of the Nephite belief system.
- **Scriptural Reference**: 1 Nephi 8 and 1 Nephi 11 – Nephi not only sees his father's vision but receives further revelations expanding on the meanings behind the symbols.

3. Redemption and Messiah

- **Characters**: Nephi, Jacob, and Isaiah
- **Theme**: The coming of Jesus Christ is a central theme articulated through the prophecies of Isaiah (2 Nephi 12-24), which Nephi reiterates and expands upon. Jacob's teachings also focus significantly on the doctrine of Jesus Christ and His atoning sacrifice.

- **Scriptural Reference**: 2 Nephi 25:26 – Nephi emphasizes the importance of prophesying of Jesus Christ as the core of their preaching.

4. Covenant and Promised Land

- **Characters**: Lehi, Nephi, and Zenos (from the Brass Plates)
- **Theme**: The concept of a covenant people and a promised land recurs throughout the narrative. Lehi's departure from Jerusalem and the subsequent journey to the promised land are portrayed as part of a divine covenant, echoed in the allegory of the olive tree by Zenos (Jacob 5).
- **Scriptural Reference**: 1 Nephi 2:20-21 – God promises Nephi that if he and his descendants keep the commandments, they shall prosper in the promised land.

5. Adversity and Deliverance

- **Characters**: Lehi, Nephi, and Sherem
- **Theme**: Throughout the Small Plates, characters frequently face adversities that test their faith and commitment. Lehi's struggles with the murmuring of his family, Nephi's challenges with his brothers, and Jacob's confrontation with Sherem (Jacob 7) highlight the theme of enduring faith leading to deliverance.

- **Scriptural Reference**: Jacob 7:5 – Jacob withstands Sherem's attempts to shake his faith, emphasizing that true faith can withstand intellectual and spiritual challenges.

6. Family Dynamics and Succession

- **Characters**: Lehi, Nephi, Laman, Lemuel, and Sam
- **Theme**: The dynamics within Lehi's family, including the rebellion of Laman and Lemuel against Nephi's leadership, underline the challenges and complexities of familial relationships and leadership succession within a covenant community.
- **Scriptural Reference**: 1 Nephi 18:15 – The description of Nephi's bound condition by his brothers shows the intense familial strife and its resolution through divine intervention.

These themes are critical for understanding the spiritual landscape of the Book of Mormon and they provide profound lessons on faith, leadership, prophecy, redemption, and perseverance applicable to contemporary readers. Each character's individual story contributes layers of meaning to these overarching themes, making the Book of Mormon a complex and rich scriptural text.

References

Church of Jesus Christ of Latter-day Saints. (2013). *Book of Mormon*. Retrieved from https://www.churchofjesuschrist.org/study/scriptures/bofm?lang=eng

Church of Jesus Christ of Latter-day Saints. (2013). *New Testament*. Retrieved from https://www.churchofjesuschrist.org/study/scriptures/nt?lang=eng

Church of Jesus Christ of Latter-day Saints. (2013). *Old Testament*. Retrieved from https://www.churchofjesuschrist.org/study/scriptures/ot?lang=eng

Church of Jesus Christ of Latter-day Saints. (2023). *Preach My Gospel: A Guide to Missionary Service: Chapter 6 - Seek Christlike Attributes*. Retrieved from https://www.churchofjesuschrist.org/study/manual/preach-my-gospel-2023/14-chapter-6?lang=eng

Matthews, R. J. (1976). *Who's Who in the Book of Mormon*. Deseret Book Company.

Pinegar, E. J., & Allen, R. J. (2007). *Book of Mormon Who's Who: Illustrated Edition, A Comprehensive Guide to the People in the Book of Mormon*. Covenant Communications, Inc.

Image References

Church of Jesus Christ of Latter-day Saints. (2024). Gospel Art: Book of Mormon. Retrieved from https://www.churchofjesus christ.org/media/collection/book-of-mormon-all-gospel-art-images?lang=eng

All images modified by the author.